TEACHING
STUDENTS
TO DECODE
THE WORLD

ascd
Alexandria, Virginia USA

Chris **SPERRY**
Cyndy **SCHEIBE**

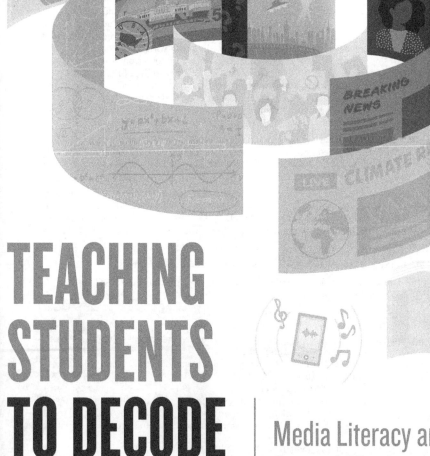

TEACHING STUDENTS TO DECODE THE WORLD

Media Literacy and
Critical Thinking
Across the Curriculum

1703 N. Beauregard St. • Alexandria, VA 22311-1714 USA
Phone: 800-933-2723 or 703-578-9600 • Fax: 703-575-5400
Website: www.ascd.org • Email: member@ascd.org
Author guidelines: www.ascd.org/write

Ranjit Sidhu, *CEO & Executive Director;* Penny Reinart, *Chief Impact Officer;* Genny Ostertag, *Managing Director, Book Acquisitions and Editing;* Susan Hills, *Senior Acquisitions Editor;* Julie Houtz, *Director, Book Editing;* Miriam Calderone, *Editor;* Thomas Lytle, *Creative Director;* Donald Ely, *Art Director;* Khanh Pham, *Graphic Designer;* Valerie Younkin, *Senior Production Designer;* Kelly Marshall, *Production Manager;* Shajuan Martin, *E-Publishing Specialist;* Christopher Logan, *Senior Production Specialist*

All web links in this book are correct as of the publication date below but may have become inactive or otherwise modified since that time. If you notice a deactivated or changed link, please email books@ascd.org with the words "Link Update" in the subject line. In your message, please specify the web link, the book title, and the page number on which the link appears.

PAPERBACK ISBN: 978-1-4166-3093-7   ASCD product #122006   n1/22

PDF E-BOOK ISBN: 978-1-4166-3094-4; see Books in Print for other formats.

Quantity discounts are available: email programteam@ascd.org or call 800-933-2723, ext. 5773, or 703-575-5773. For desk copies, go to www.ascd.org/deskcopy.

Library of Congress Cataloging-in-Publication Data
Names: Sperry, Chris, author. | Scheibe, Cyndy, author.
Title: Teaching students to decode the world : media literacy and critical thinking across the curriculum / Chris Sperry and Cyndy Scheibe.
Description: Alexandria, VA : ASCD, 2022. | Includes bibliographical references and index.
Identifiers: LCCN 2021046019 (print) | LCCN 2021046020 (ebook) | ISBN 9781416630937 (paperback) | ISBN 9781416630944 (pdf)
Subjects: LCSH: Media literacy—Study and teaching (Elementary) | Media literacy—Study and teaching (Secondary) | Critical thinking—Study and teaching (Elementary) | Critical thinking—Study and teaching (Secondary) | Interdisciplinary approach in education. | Constructivism (Education)
Classification: LCC P96.M4 S66 2022 (print) | LCC P96.M4 (ebook) | DDC 302.23071—dc23/eng/20211115
LC record available at https://lccn.loc.gov/2021046019
LC ebook record available at https://lccn.loc.gov/2021046020

31 30 29 28 27 26 25 24 23 22   1 2 3 4 5 6 7 8 9 10 11 12

TEACHING STUDENTS TO DECODE THE WORLD
Media Literacy and Critical Thinking Across the Curriculum

ACKNOWLEDGMENTS

For 25 years, we have been inspired and supported by more people than we can possibly name here, including the many teachers and librarians who have worked with Project Look Sharp and the incredible media literacy educators across the nation from whom we have learned so much. Our ongoing collaboration with Faith Rogow—an outstanding author and advocate for media literacy in the lives of young children—has been especially important; she is the first person we call when we need advice, and her unwavering support for our work is so deeply appreciated.

We owe an enormous debt of gratitude to our colleagues at Project Look Sharp whose work is strongly reflected in this book, especially long-time curriculum writer, mentor, friend, and brother, Sox Sperry. We also appreciate those at Ithaca College who have strongly supported media literacy integration and the growth of Project Look Sharp's work both on and off campus, including the development of the first interdisciplinary media literacy minor in the United States.

We especially want to thank our editor, Susan Hills, who approached us at an ASCD conference to propose this book, and who would not give up on this project even when we thought the copyright restrictions around media examples would make it impossible. Her support and feedback helped make this a much better book.

For decades, our students at Ithaca College and the Lehman Alternative Community School have provided both the inspiration and the continual feedback that made this work possible. Without their insights and trust, we could not have developed this approach to teaching and learning.

INTRODUCTION

Our Origin Stories

Chris's story: If it had not been for my dad's Super 8 movie camera, I would not have become a teacher. My teenage experiences making surfing films at the Jersey Shore brought me to college to make movies and then to teach media production at the Lehman Alternative Community School, a progressive public school in Ithaca, New York, where I taught for more than 40 years. The personal empowerment that came with creating and reading media as a teenager enabled me to see myself as a capable communicator. It also helped me to see the capacity in all my students—and prompted me to craft instructional modalities that were accessible to more students. My students provided the inspiration and the continual feedback that made this work possible. Without their insights and trust, we could not have developed this approach to teaching and learning.

Cyndy's story: I first came to media literacy through the mentorship of Professor John Condry when I was a graduate student at Cornell University. John and I were both influenced by FCC commissioner Nicholas Johnson's statement that "All television is educational television. The question is: what is it teaching?" (Condry, 1989). We started a research lab and archive to study changes in television content over time, interviewing children to assess their understanding of program content and commercials. When I gave talks to parents and teachers, they always wanted to know what could be done to limit the harmful effects of television, and it was through my later collaboration with Faith Rogow that I came to understand that instead of protecting children, we needed to empower them with skills in critical thinking and media literacy.

The two of us met through our daughters, Alexis and Ariana, who were in the same kindergarten class, and quickly discovered our mutual interest in the relatively new field of media literacy. In 1996, we founded Project Look Sharp, a largely grant-funded initiative at Ithaca College, where Cyndy is a professor of developmental psychology and where Chris graduated from in 1979 with an independent cross-disciplinary major in media literacy. From the start, Project Look Sharp's mission was to support educators—first locally, then regionally, and now across the globe—in integrating media literacy and critical thinking into their teaching.

Project Look Sharp and Our Approach

Shortly after we founded Project Look Sharp, we decided to focus our work on the topic of this book—constructivist media decoding (CMD)—with a strong emphasis on critical thinking and reflection. We initially viewed our primary role as providing professional development using resources created by experts in media literacy. But our ongoing conversations with teachers and librarians led us to two conclusions. First, the successful integration of media literacy into K–12 classrooms required a *curriculum-driven* approach, with lessons that taught core content along with media literacy skills. Second, educators needed free and easy access to media literacy lessons and media examples that they could use (or adapt) in their classes.

Over the past two decades, Project Look Sharp has gradually built a repository of more than 500 question-based media literacy lessons and activities (including more than 2,000 media examples provided through the fair use exemption to copyright laws), searchable by keyword, grade level, subject area, and learning standard. All these resources—along with handouts, journal articles, and video demonstrations of constructivist media decoding with elementary, high school, and college students—are available at no charge for educators through our website, www.project lookatsharp.org.

About This Book

This book is our attempt to codify the theory, process, and pedagogical complexities of question-based media analysis in the classroom, providing a road map for educators to develop CMD activities of their own. Although it is written for K–12 teachers, librarians, educational leaders, preservice teachers, and media literacy advocates, we believe it will be useful for anyone interested in teaching students of all ages to "decode the world."

The opening chapter lays out the imperatives for doing this work. Chapter 2 introduces the key frameworks for understanding media literacy, critical thinking, and constructivist media decoding (CMD). Chapter 3 gets readers started with the basics of developing and leading a CMD activity in the classroom, and Chapter 4 goes into greater detail on the specifics of the methodology and implementation. Chapter 5 delves into issues of bias, teaching challenging topics, and students' meaning making, and Chapter 6 explores assessment and metacognition as they relate to CMD. Chapter 7 looks at pedagogical connections between CMD and other educational initiatives and approaches, including media production, project-based learning, social-emotional learning, cultural competency, and antiracist education. The final chapter explores how to integrate CMD across a school or district and ends with the voices of teachers and students about the impact of this work on their teaching and learning.

The bulk of this book is written in the first-person plural, with *we* referring to the collective voice of Cyndy and Chris, although at times we will tell stories from our individual experiences. It's important to note at the outset that, although we cannot separate our voices and perspectives from the biases that are reflected in our identities, we have done our best to stay mindful of our own backgrounds, to avoid letting the assumptions and biases rooted in those backgrounds create blind spots in our guidance for educators, and to create a book that is inclusive of other perspectives and appropriately contextualized in the current sociopolitical climate that affects students, schools, and learning. We are both White, middle-class, liberal, cisgender, highly educated parents and grandparents, having grown up in the 1960s and '70s, and now living in Ithaca, New York. Chris taught in a public school for more than 40 years. Cyndy has been a college professor for more than 30 years and has a daughter, a son-in-law, and grandchildren who are Peruvian–African American. These identities have shaped our views, our approaches to teaching, and the narrative that is this book.

We want to make special note of our capitalization of the word *White* when referring to race. The word *Black* is often capitalized when referring to Black people (Black culture, Black community, and more). This is typically not true for the word *White,* except in the writings of White supremacists who seek to elevate Whiteness to a proper noun. In this book, we have chosen to capitalize racial references to Whiteness for a very different reason. At the core of systemic racism is the invisibility of Whiteness, the unspoken acceptance that Whiteness is the norm and therefore does not need to be named in our language. By capitalizing *White,* we continually remind ourselves that our history, our educational systems, our perspectives, and our language have biases—especially when it comes to race. We want to credit Kwame Anthony Appiah (2020) for his writing on this subject.

Historical Context

The other critical context that has shaped our writing is the historical moment we are living through. As we were writing this book, we were in the midst of a global pandemic that shut down schools and forced online learning across the planet. We were also emerging from four years of a Trump presidency that was accompanied by a surge in political polarization, driven in part by changes in media technology and economics. This situation has fed an epistemological crisis regarding what constitutes "truth" that will far outlive this moment. The summer of 2020 also saw historic protests against White supremacy and for racial equality that are pushing the United States to confront powerful and divisive questions about its history and future. And the raging fires, hurricanes, floods, and droughts of recent years highlight the global climate crisis that will define our children's future.

We intend for this book—while practical and applied to the realities of today's classrooms—to be useful in negotiating these big issues with students. We aim for this work to be not only steeped in the imperatives of our moment but also fundamentally grounded in the universal and perennial themes of good teaching. Most importantly, we hope that the resources, methodologies, tips, and stories we share will help educators in their idealistic work to raise generations prepared to tackle the awesome task of human progress.

THE IMPERATIVES OF
MEDIA LITERACY TODAY

During the 2011–12 school year, we delivered a series of trainings for teams of librarians and science teachers to support the integration of media literacy and critical thinking into elementary science. At the third and final meeting of the group in March, we heard the following story from one of the teams. After the initial daylong training in September, the elementary teacher had turned to her librarian colleague and said, "What do these people think I am supposed to do with my 1st graders? My 6-year-olds can't do the kind of critical thinking they are proposing." The librarian had responded brilliantly: "Well, let's see what we might do." She then asked the teacher about her class, her greatest challenges, and her next unit. The teacher explained that she was struggling with a number of boys who seemed to be interested only in violent superheroes. Her next science unit was on matter: liquid, solid, and gas. The librarian went to work looking for the right media document.

A few days later, the librarian showed the teacher a 30-second clip from a Marvel video, *Spider-Man vs. Hydro-Man*. They decided to use it for pre- and post-assessments for the unit on matter. They showed the clip and asked students what was accurate (or true) and what was inaccurate (or not true) in what the video showed about liquids. In the pre-assessment, the students had no idea. But at the end of the unit, the class was able to give evidence-based responses that demonstrated their understanding of the properties of liquid. In the discussion, one student explained, "Hydro-Man walks around just made of water. That's wrong because we learned that liquid takes on the shape of whatever it is in." Another student chimed in with "the vessel." And another response was "But after Hydro-Man turns into a puddle, we see the sun heats him up and he begins to evaporate." Another student said, "That can happen because a liquid can turn into a gas when it gets too hot."

The teacher was delighted that the 1st graders were able to apply their content learning from the unit to the analysis of popular culture. But then the teacher went on to do the kind of media literacy questioning she had learned in the training by asking, "So, you are telling me that the *Spider-Man* video shows things that are not true—not accurate science? Why would the makers of the video do that?" One student responded, "They didn't make the video to teach us real science; they made it to be fun." After some discussion about the purpose of movies and TV shows, the teacher asked, "So what does this exercise teach us about what we need to do when we watch TV?" After a pause, a student said, "We need to be careful not to believe everything we see on TV because not everything on TV is made to be real."

The most exciting part of the story is what the teacher shared during the debriefing at our final professional development session. She was shocked by her 1st graders' ability to think so abstractly. This teacher was an experienced and accomplished educator, yet she—like all of us—was subject to prior assumptions and expectations about her students. Other teachers who participated in that series of media literacy trainings shared the same realization:

- "Children can be stretched even further than I expected. They need to be given the opportunity to think and express themselves using concrete information to support their ideas."

- "[From now on] I will not be afraid to let my students *think*. Too often I direct their thinking to get to the goal I want them to reach. I will let them explore and think more critically about what I am teaching."

One of the most important reasons to practice question-based media analysis with students is to bring forward their impressive abilities to teach one another complex understandings from their own developmental place. Another reason for this work is to give all students access to the power of literacy and critical thinking. In the words of a 10th grade student when speaking about the impact of media literacy, "It made me realize just how much power people have to change or control things, for better or worse. I, however, am not passive to this change. I can be a part of it and affect it."

Enfranchising All Students

Educators who have been trained in this type of inquiry-based media analysis—what we call *constructivist media decoding*, or CMD—regularly comment on the high level of student engagement in the process. They describe how media decoding brings forward the views of traditionally quiet or disengaged students. Here are a few quotes from the teachers who participated in the initiative for integrating media literacy into the K–12 science curriculum:

- "The kids stayed on and continued the discussion after the bell rang."
- "This got students involved who have no intrinsic motivation."
- "It really helps students use a different part of their brain than they're used to using at school!"
- "Even my 'trouble' students raised their hands and had good comments!"

The last observation struck a personal chord for Chris. He describes himself as having been one of those "trouble" students, in part because he was a terrible speller. Although he was deeply curious about ideas, he could not—and still can't—keep track of the letters in words. This simple difference in orientation led Chris to believe that he was "stupid." And when one feels stupid in school, it is typically a torturous place to spend six hours a day. When a middle-class White boy in the 1960s, with lots of privilege, can become alienated from school because he's a poor speller, it's no wonder that millions of students without those advantages can feel deeply challenged in traditional classrooms.

One of the primary imperatives for incorporating media literacy into the classroom is the personal empowerment of students. By diversifying the types of texts we use in school—using engaging popular-culture documents for complex classroom analysis, ensuring that we include texts that reflect a variety of perspectives, and varying the modalities we use for assessment and instruction—we enhance the capacity for a greater diversity of students to feel that school is an empowering place. When we do that, all students learn better.

In 1979, when Chris began teaching at the Lehman Alternative Community School (LACS), a progressive public school in Ithaca, New York, he was confronted by the challenge of choosing texts. His wonderful little school drew a broad range of students—and they knew it. On one side of the room, the children of Cornell University and Ithaca College professors, typically confident (or at least comfortable) with academics, sat together. On the other side of the room sat students who, in many cases, came from families for whom school had rarely been empowering. Both groups had multigenerational experience with success or failure linked to the process of schooling.

And at the heart of that experience was the printed word. Chris could see it in their body language when he handed out a reading. The "academic" students were typically interested and intellectually critical. But his alienated students, many from rural and less educated backgrounds, showed discomfort and even anger. When Chris made texts simpler, the change backfired and increased the polarization in the room, as students took offense at the notion that he had "dumbed things down." As someone who learned to read through the pictures in comic books and who became a confident communicator through making films about surfing, Chris could empathize with the discomfort of his disgruntled students. More importantly, he could see their brilliance despite their challenges with "traditional" academics.

Diversifying Texts

In this context, Chris turned to the very options that provided the key to his own success in school: diverse media forms. He began bringing in photographs and paintings to teach history, video and film clips to teach geography, songs and stories to communicate cultural and historical perspectives. Although he used these various kinds of texts to teach and reinforce social studies knowledge and concepts, he also asked students to analyze the texts: "Who made this and for what purpose?" "What is their perspective and bias, and where do you see it in the document?"

Although Chris first began using question-based media analysis in his media production classes, he soon incorporated it into his social studies and English classes to teach core content as well as critical-thinking skills. This approach made learning more engaging for all of Chris's students and leveled the classroom playing field. In fact, many of Chris's students who were the biggest media consumers were often better at analyzing popular-culture messages than their more "academic" peers. For all of the students, it was more fun to engage in a rigorous task—analyzing engaging media documents—than to passively take in the instruction.

In the 1990s, when Chris and Cyndy began training teachers in this approach, the educators shared other reasons why the repurposing of media texts to teach content and literacy was so important. They spoke about how the process connected to the "real lives" of students and prepared them for life in our hypermediated world (even in the 1990s). They saw how it could effectively integrate the teaching of literacy skills and subject-area knowledge and concepts through inquiry. They appreciated its adaptability for use as lesson prompts, for brief activities, for core instruction, and as assessments. And they gravitated to this process for teaching controversial and emotional topics that benefited from an evidence-based analytical approach.

Developing Habits of Questioning

Today's students have grown up in a mediated world quite different from that of their teachers and the younger students who will follow them. Two constants for all these cohorts are a growth in new media forms and an increase in youth media consumption. Although we cannot know the kinds of media forms that will be ubiquitous for the next generation of students, we can anticipate the skills, attitudes, and habits that will better equip them to have agency in their mediated lives. Students then (as now) will need to recognize the constructed nature of media messages. They will need to continually reflect on the meanings and effects of the media messages they consume, share, and create. They will need to think critically about the forms of media as well as the content. They will need to habitually ask critical questions about authorship, sourcing, credibility, and bias. And they will need to reflect on their own thinking about these messages— and their own preconceived notions—as they negotiate truth in a hypermediated world.

To become internalized, these skills and attitudes need to be continually repeated, at all grade levels and in multiple curricular areas. Media literacy needs to be integrated across the curriculum. The crush of new curricular mandates and content makes this goal seem impossible, but the approach to media literacy advocated in this book is methodological. It advocates the repurposing of textbooks, videos, websites, and all the diverse media we use to teach our curriculum to also teach critical thinking and media literacy.

Teaching our students to think critically about mediated messages must not be limited to the most sophisticated higher-order thinking skills relegated to upper-level high school and college classes. We often hear that this work needs to wait until students have the core background knowledge and sophistication that will enable them to think critically. That view is like saying that we should aim to teach students to read when they are ready to handle Shakespeare. As was indicated in the earlier *Spider-Man vs. Hydro-Man* example, even young students are capable of thinking critically about authorship, purpose, credibility, and bias—at their own level. Developing these habits cannot wait. It is at the heart of learning.

Media, Literacy, and Democracy

It is important to note that U.S. copyright law also plays a major role in supporting this work in schools. In some countries, teachers are not allowed to repurpose copyrighted media documents (video clips, images, songs, etc.) because of restrictive copyright laws. In the United States, copyright law includes a *fair use* clause, an underappreciated policy that enables critical thinking for the nation's democracy. Currently the fair use doctrine allows the repurposing of copyrighted material for critique and criticism in an educational context without permission from the copyright owner. Therefore, fair use gives educators the right to repurpose media messages in the classroom. Democracy gives us the responsibility to do this continually.

When the founders of American democracy debated about the culture that was necessary to shift from monarchy to rule by citizens, they discussed literacy, education, and the media. They decided not to establish a government newspaper, arguing that was what the British monarchy had done. Instead, they agreed to subsidize the delivery of newspapers to all interested citizens. The postal subsidy was created in part to enable the political media of the day—newspapers—to reach all U.S. citizens. And these papers were overtly political. Most newspapers for the first 80 years of the nation's history were linked to, if not directly controlled by, political parties (Starr, 2004). The founders recognized that wide-ranging political debate through the media was a core component of democracy.

The founders also recognized that democracy was dependent on an electorate that was capable of understanding the conflicting and complex issues of the day. In 1817, Thomas Jefferson wrote, "An enlightened citizenry is indispensable for the proper functioning of a republic. Self-government is not possible unless the citizens are educated sufficiently to enable them to exercise oversight" (Arthur, Davies, & Hahn, 2008, p. 403). Within the origins of the United States, the links among literacy, public education, and democracy were drawn.

At the same time, issues of power and control were explicitly connected to literacy, public education, and democracy. After the slave revolt led by Nat Turner in 1831, it became illegal to teach an African American to read and write in most slave states. Frederick Douglass is often quoted as saying, "Once you learn to read, you will be forever free" (Wright, 2019, p. 1). Although the founders saw literacy as essential to democracy, the systems they created denied both literacy and democracy to specific groups of citizens. Today, media literacy can play an enfranchising role in empowering *all* students to experience the freeing power of 21st century literacy.

Causes of an Infodemic

According to the World Health Organization (2020), in addition to being in the midst of a terrible pandemic, "we are also in the midst of a massive global 'Infodemic': an overabundance of information—some accurate and some not—that makes it hard for people to find trustworthy sources and reliable guidance when they need it" (p. 2). We are living in a time when one group's fake news is another group's certainty, when facts have become arbitrary, and when our identities determine our truths. This epistemological chasm has great implications for democracy and for media literacy. Media—both the messages and the forms of communication—play an ever more important role in shaping public consciousness. It is worth taking the space to explore the mediated factors that led us to this infodemic (Sperry & Scheibe, 2020).

Throughout the second half of the 20th century, the medium of television was a dominant force in public meaning making, especially about political ideas. Radio, the medium that brought voice into living rooms and gave Americans their first "personal president" (Franklin D. Roosevelt), was replaced by a medium dominated by mass-produced images and sound bites. Television, with its emphasis on *looking* good, paved the way for John F. Kennedy. In 1960, the young first-term senator defeated a sitting vice president in a close election that may have turned on the first televised presidential debates. If the election had been a decade earlier, before TV had replaced radio as the primary news medium, the result of the election might have been different. The election of 1960 reminds us of Marshall McLuhan's famous saying, "The medium is the message" (McLuhan, 1994, p. 7).

The 1980s then brought Ronald Reagan, "the great communicator," to the White House. Reagan's principal media advisor, Michael Deaver, said, "People absorb impressions rather than substance, particularly in this day and age"; and Reagan, with his background as a film and TV actor, knew all about impressions (PBS, 1999). When Reagan was introduced to the team that created his famous "Morning in America" ads for the 1980 presidential election campaign, the future president said, "If you're going to sell soap, you ought to see the bar" (Beschloss, 2016, p. 4). Reagan understood that victory would come through selling the right impressions of him—and America—through the medium of TV.

It is important to note that the tendency of the electorate to vote for the candidate who has the best handle on the dominant media of the day preceded the modern era. The 1840 "campaign as spectacle" used parades, sloganeering, popular song, and the *Log Cabin* newspaper (along with lots of free booze) to enlist the newly enfranchised White farming men of the American West (e.g., Ohio) to vote for William Henry Harrison. Horace Greeley, Harrison's campaign manager, successfully spun an impression of a hard-drinking working man despite the fact that Harrison was a 68-year-old Washington, D.C., aristocrat (Shafer, 2016).

Fast-forward to 2016, when Donald Trump used his experience with reality TV to dominate both traditional and social media. Despite significant negative coverage, his ability to break through the clutter and galvanize his base vaulted him to the White House, where he broke many norms of presidential behavior, including through the continuous renunciation of facts. Although much of the mainstream media played its traditional role as fact checker, much of the country had changed along with its media. The advent of the internet and social media enabled Trump to delegitimize mainstream news (at least for his base) and to present "alternative facts" that reflected his and their views of reality. The shift from the airways to fiber-optic communication, from the *New York Times* to Twitter, and from Walter Cronkite to Tucker Carlson, helped create the presidency of Donald Trump.

Politics, Filter Bubbles, and Echo Chambers

Broadcast television in the mid-20th century, with its limited number of news channels, needed a huge viewership to be competitive. The ABC, NBC, and CBS networks vied for the attention of the nation by catering to the political middle. The economies of scale in broadcast news helped marginalize "extreme" perspectives as an ethos of "objective" journalism helped keep alternative views out of the mainstream. That situation began to change in the 1980s and '90s, as talk radio and then cable news segmented viewers (and advertising dollars) into factions. The stoking of political and identity-based rage and resentment found new platforms with the advent of the internet. As with traditional media, drama and conflict held eyeballs; but new algorithms, driven by advertising dollars, nudged web users toward more outrageous views. Social media provided the ideal vehicle for propelling polarized politics. Users could now consume news 24/7 through "filter bubbles" that reflected their passions, delegitimized contrary viewpoints, and continually reinforced their views, creating "echo chambers." This segmenting of our media ecology has had a profound impact on how we perceive truth and those who disagree with our views.

Pause to Reflect

What are your mediated filter bubbles? How do they affect how you see the world? Are you part of any echo chambers? How does this influence how you see (and relate to) those who think differently than you do?

Many other factors contributed to the election of Donald Trump and the identity-fueled polarization of U.S. politics, but changes in media technology and economics have clearly fed the division of citizens into like-minded echo chambers of belief. In our current infodemic, scientific facts are trumped by cultural and political identities, news can become "fake" if it falls outside one's ideological orientation, and truly fake news (disinformation) can spread virally inside filter bubbles. Although policy decisions and technology fixes may help to limit the impact of this threat to American democracy, we must also use the tools of the Enlightenment (e.g., reason and science) to develop an educated citizenry.

Schools—and public schools in particular—are charged with educating a literate population that is capable of negotiating the barrage of expertly crafted spin, partisan propaganda, and outright lies that characterize U.S. politics. This effort must involve teaching students to understand the role of media in crafting messages—political and otherwise. It must involve slowing down the relentless flood of mediated messages so that young people can begin to take a critical look at the craft of spinning information. It must involve helping students to understand how each media form has its own unique language of construction and its own biases. It must involve helping students to separate impressions from substance and truth from lies. And it must involve helping young people to reflect on the role that their own biases play in determining what they believe to be true. This infodemic within an era of fake news makes it ever clearer that authentic democracy requires us to habitually ask critical questions about all media messages and continually reflect on our own biases.

Thinking About Thinking

In 2017, Joseph Kahne and Benjamin Bowyer published a study of how young people distinguish truth from misinformation in claims about controversial issues. What they found should cause educators to rethink their approach to teaching facts. The researchers disaggregated students with high levels of political knowledge and interest from students with little or none. Common sense would suggest that students who had a lot of knowledge about the subject at hand would be better able to assess true claims and spot misinformation about them. Instead, the study revealed that students who knew a lot of relevant information on the subjects in question were no better able to distinguish truth from fiction than students who knew very little. If our top students—who are highly motivated to learn and who do well on tests—are no better at epistemological assessments than our least informed and engaged students, then we need to rethink our curriculum.

As you may have already guessed, one reason that knowledge alone does not enable students to effectively evaluate truth claims in political media is *confirmation bias*—the tendency to seek out, validate, and share information and sources that align with one's views and to dismiss arguments and sources that present opposing views. (In the study just described, students with deeply held political convictions used their knowledge to justify their reasoning about the truthfulness of news.) More facts, including all the important information we fill students with during class time, are unlikely to sway their motivated reasoning toward verifiable facts. But there are ways to help these students—and their less motivated peers—to become better at identifying truth amid misinformation and disinformation.

Kahne and Bowyer studied a range of media literacy programs to assess if they succeeded in helping students more accurately judge truth claims. They found that successful initiatives shared an emphasis on metacognition. Curricula that gave students practice in recognizing and reflecting on their own confirmation biases helped them become better able to evaluate truth claims in the media. Any curriculum that aims to address the epistemological crisis that confronts our culture needs to teach students of all ages to practice thinking about their own thinking.

Rx for an Infodemic

We propose that media literacy, and in particular the use of constructivist media decoding in the classroom, can be a key to fighting the epistemological virus that is threatening U.S. democracy. By teaching our students, from the earliest grades and throughout their schooling, to ask key questions about all media messages, we can prepare them to navigate this world of hyperpolarized politics that spin reality and twist truth. By helping them to develop the habits of critical thinking, we can provide the orientations needed for authentic participation in democracy. By repurposing all types of media messages for critical analysis, we can teach students to have agency in their thinking and their actions. This work aligns with the greatest ideals of liberal education, but it is also solidly situated in the everyday realities of the K–12 public school classroom.

A 10th grade student summed up this view after doing media decoding activities as part of a social studies class: "It is enormously important to learn about the world from many different viewpoints, approaching life with critical thinking and an open mind. We can only really solve problems when we come at them with an open mind. And we can only solve problems if we aren't afraid to think."

This book intends to be practical and to provide accessible strategies for integrating media analysis across the curriculum. We developed this approach through our own experience as teachers and, most importantly, our decades-long work that has included listening to educators who sought to effectively integrate media literacy into their teaching. As a result, it responds to the very real constraints of time: time in the curriculum, time during the day, and time for preparation. It addresses the importance of standards, subjects, and assessment. It attempts to address the importance of equity, social-emotional learning, and cultural competence. It builds on the work of project-based learning, Understanding by Design, authentic assessment, and other essential practices in contemporary education. And it aims to translate our highest aspirations for learning and social transformation into doable, realistic, and practiced methodologies.

The practical methodology of leading question-based media analysis in the classroom models a pedagogical shift from viewing teaching as the expert delivery of information to seeing teaching as the artful facilitation of the learning process. In the 40 years that the two of us have been teaching, a digital revolution in mediated information has necessitated this profound transformation. Our students no longer need their teachers or librarians to give them access to facts, but they do need us to teach them how to *navigate* the overwhelming and relentless overabundance of information. Our classrooms provide the platform for nurturing shared meaning making, where students with more complex understandings can provoke growth in the thinking of their peers.

To guide this learning, we must know our students well, both individually and collectively. We can facilitate discussions, probe with questions, provoke deliberation, and assess learning in order to help our students grapple with progressively more complex understandings of the world and themselves. Although the methodology presented here may be discrete in its application (that is, the decoding of media messages), it has deep implications for how we see teaching and learning.

At the heart of this work is the belief in the brilliance and the personal empowerment of each of our students. At the heart of this work is the essential role of media literacy in authentic democracy. At the heart of this work is the role that inquiry, reflection, and action play in being fully human.

Brazilian educator Paulo Freire (1970, 1985) wrote most powerfully about the intersection of literacy and power. For Freire, it was essential for humans to learn to decode the social messages that either reinforce the power structure or challenge it. Literacy is a prerequisite for human liberation—for reaching our full potential in the world. At the heart of that process is asking questions about the constructed nature of power. At no time in human history has the importance of literacy—and specifically media literacy—been more evident.

THE FOUNDATIONS OF CONSTRUCTIVIST MEDIA DECODING (CMD)

The focus of this book is the highly interactive educational practice of integrating constructivist media decoding throughout the curriculum. First, however, we need to ground our conversation in a common understanding of some basic principles of media literacy and critical thinking, and that starts with expanding our conception of what is meant by "media."

What Do We Mean by "Media"?

When we do professional development sessions with educators, we often start with the "morning media" activity described in the "Pause to Reflect" box on the following page. This generating of lists of possible media forms precedes our providing a definition of "media" to work from. Right off the bat, this activity models the constructivist, inquiry-based approach that we use throughout the CMD practice. And it's a great activity to do with students—especially at the beginning of the school year—to engage them in idea generation and collective process.

Pause to Reflect

From the moment you woke up this morning until right now, what are all of the different kinds of media that you've used or been exposed to? Jot them down, and then think about the commonalities across the items on your list that would cause you to think of them as all falling into the category of "media." How many of them would be considered "digital media"? How many of them might be considered "traditional media"—forms that have been around for 50 years or more? How would your list differ from the list that your students might make?

Like the CMD process in general, activities such as this inform us about our students' experience, providing a window into the media worlds they are living in today. It may challenge our assumptions about the types of media our students are using and provide insights into the range of media used across students of the same age. Research by Common Sense Media (2015, 2019), for example, has identified different types of media users among tweens and teens—including social networkers (mostly girls), video gamers (mostly boys), heavy media users (spending many hours, using different forms), light media users, readers, and media makers. The activity can also serve as a stepping-stone for developing a definition of "media" that applies to very old media forms (such as paintings, carvings, drumming, and money), along with current media forms and those yet to be developed.

If you're like most people today, you probably had social media on your list—which at the time of this writing (in fall 2021) might include Twitter, Facebook, YouTube, LinkedIn, Instagram, Snapchat, TikTok, and more—and your students might be likely to name those forms of media first. Social media are inherently interactive, connecting people through commentary and the sharing of images, sound, and video content. Today's social media are also inherently digital, requiring some kind of device (cell phone, tablet, computer) that uses technology to mediate the message between individuals and groups—which is a key part of what makes something "media."

Those forms of digital media—along with internet websites and apps—have become increasingly prevalent and important parts of virtually everyone's lives today. They are central to much of formal and informal education and are required for most occupations as well. Fluency in digital technologies has now moved to early elementary grades, and "digital health" is a growing field that encompasses everything from online etiquette and cyberbullying to finding online resources dealing with physical and mental health issues.

However, not all forms of media are necessarily digital. You probably included some type of television on your list, which is still the most frequently used media form across all age groups—although the platform is now likely to include content from many cable stations viewed on hand-held devices as well as on traditional TV sets. You might also have included newspapers, magazines, films, and something like radio (which today might include podcasts, and music from digital platforms such as Spotify or Pandora). If you are a gamer, you probably included video or computer games. You might have included advertising (which comes in many different forms and is embedded in most other types of media) and things such as photographs, comics, games, bumper stickers, T-shirts, or food packaging. But did you include books?

We often don't think about books as media. It's not clear why we don't. Perhaps it's because, as educators, we often think of "media" as inherently bad for children and teens, something that we need to guard against in the classroom. But books—including book covers and textbooks—are still one of the main forms of media used in education, and it's important to apply the principles of media analysis to the content of books and other forms of media (including posters and maps) that we commonly use in our classrooms.

Although definitions vary across disciplines, when we talk about "media," we focus on messages with the following characteristics:

- *Conveyed through language, visuals, and/or sound*
- *Mediated* (produced and shared) *through some form of technology*
- Typically (although not always) *mass produced for a mass audience*

For most media messages, the person who created the message is not in the same physical space as the receiver of the message. That aspect is important, because it means that it's much easier for the message to be manipulated (through editing, cropping, digital distortion, etc.) than is the case in face-to-face communication. It also means that the communication is often one-way, and the feedback loop is absent or indirect (through posting comments, writing letters to the editor, etc.). When we are communicating in person—including in the classroom with our students, or even when using synchronous online teaching methods—we can ask questions, probe for clarification and understanding, and pay attention to the facial expressions and body language of those receiving our message. That is not usually the case for creators of media messages.

What makes something "media" is not always straightforward. For instance, traditional letters and phone calls would typically not be considered because they are person-to-person communication; but when a letter is published in a newspaper or on the internet and is communicated to a mass audience, or when a robocall goes out to hundreds of people, then those messages do become media. Live music, storytelling, and dance are not mass produced or mediated by technology, but the lyrics, storyline, and choreography are often components of mass media. Social media and other new forms of digital communication often blur the boundaries between direct person-to-person communication and mass media.

The critical point is that more and more of our message making and receiving has moved from relatively direct communication to increasingly complex systems of mass communication. This shift has had an increasing influence on how we create, share, and understand social messages. And it is one of the reasons why it's so important to have students practice decoding (deconstructing) mediated messages, especially in a classroom setting where we can unpack the different interpretations that students may have of the same media message.

What Do We Mean by "Media Literacy"?

Given this broad interpretation of "media," encompassing both traditional (print) and more recent (digital) forms of media, the concept of media literacy is really quite simple: extending literacy—reading and writing—to apply to all of those forms and technologies through which we get information, ideas, impressions, and entertainment. This *grounding of media literacy as literacy* in today's world is fundamental to the approaches applied in this book. It highlights the importance of developing media literacy skills across grade levels and practicing those skills as matters of habit in all curriculum areas.

The most common definitions of media literacy in the United States emphasize "the ability to *access, analyze, evaluate*, and *produce* communication in a variety of forms" (Aufderheide, 1993, p. 5). Although today most organizations use *create* rather than *produce*, these four elements are broadly accepted as core to media literacy education. A fifth element— *taking action*—is now typically incorporated into the definition as well (Hobbs, 2010b; NAMLE, 2020). Some in the field have highlighted other elements as core to media literacy, including *participation* (Jenkins, 2009), *collaboration* (Friesem, 2014), and *reflection* (Scheibe & Rogow, 2012). A number of researchers and theorists use the term *critical media literacy* to emphasize issues of power, equity, and justice in the media, particularly corporate media (Alvermann & Hagood, 2010; Funk, Kellner, & Share, 2016).

The graphic developed by Project Look Sharp (see Figure 2.1) represents our view of the process of media literacy. It incorporates the five most widely accepted elements of media literacy—*access, analysis, evaluation, creation,* and *action*—while emphasizing the interactive nature of those components. It also highlights the importance of *inquiry and reflection* as central to the whole process of media literacy; they are core to critical thinking and are the basis for key questions to ask when analyzing (and creating) media messages—questions that will be discussed later in the book.

FIGURE 2.1 **The Media Literacy Process**

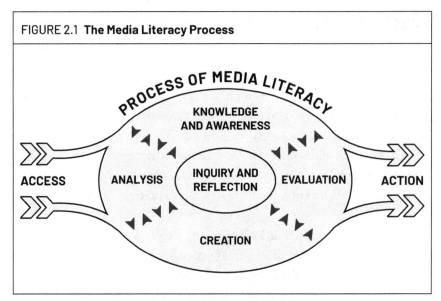

Source: © 2014 Project Look Sharp. Used with permission.

This graphic identifies *access* as the predecessor for the process of media literacy, representing access to both media (you can't learn to read without having books or other reading material) and media literacy education. Access is an important part of information literacy, including having the skills and the tools to search for information without censorship and to use those tools effectively and ethically. This issue of access is often taken for granted in the United States, but it is heavily influenced by various forms of systemic discrimination (including those based on race and social class), and it certainly applies in the K–12 classroom, where some media content may be blocked from student use. During the time of the coronavirus pandemic, access to the internet and educational technologies was a huge challenge for many students at all grade levels (including college students), reinforcing the importance of access as essential for education and many aspects of daily life.

Although media literacy is largely a set of skills and abilities, the Project Look Sharp graphic shown in Figure 2.1 includes *knowledge and awareness* as a key component to the process of media literacy. This includes knowledge about how different types of media messages are created, and the vocabulary used to describe the components and techniques used in different media formats (e.g., *pace, jump cut, pan, zoom, extreme close-up, scrolling* in film and video content; *headline, caption, framing, Photoshopping* in print news and still images; *URL, wallpaper, banner, pop-up* in apps and websites). It also includes knowledge about how media industries work, how they are regulated, and issues of consolidated ownership across many media outlets. And it includes a heightened awareness of one's own media use, and of the effects of media messages on people of different ages and backgrounds, on society, and on the democratic process.

Analysis and evaluation are the main focus of this book and of the constructivist media decoding process, so we will be talking about them extensively in later chapters. *Analysis* involves decoding the messages that are seen, heard, and read by asking key questions about how and why particular messages were constructed, including deconstructing the techniques used to convey the messages. *Evaluation* involves making informed, reasoned judgments about the value and utility of messages for different purposes and different audiences. Evaluation includes reflecting on the credibility, accuracy, and currency of the information presented; how well the media maker(s) used the techniques to inform, entertain, or persuade; and how the messages might affect the recipient and others. More than any other components of media literacy, analysis and evaluation rely heavily on critical thinking and the ongoing practices of questioning and reflection.

Although not the focus of this book, we readily acknowledge the importance of *creation* in media literacy, and in Chapter 7 we will discuss how students can build on their constructivist media decoding skills to make their own media messages—and how they can gain powerful insights about the messages created by others (newscasters, advertisers, politicians, etc.) by doing so. The difference between just making media and making media through the lens of media literacy involves reflection—taking the time to think about the goals in making the message, about the target audience and the techniques used to reach it, about what to include and what to leave out (and how that might affect the message), and about how the media creation might affect people who see, hear, or read the message. These considerations apply to any kind of media message, including a tweet or a TikTok video, a poster created to hold up during a demonstration, a PowerPoint presentation for a school project, an article for a school newspaper, or a public service announcement to highlight a critical health issue.

In the same way that *access* is the precursor to media literacy, *action* represents the outcome. Without the ability to take actions based on the media literacy skills a student has developed, media literacy would remain an academic exercise. Paulo Freire (1970) describes *praxis* as the synthesis of theory and practice. In his seminal work, *Pedagogy of the Oppressed,* Freire wrote, "Knowledge emerges only through invention and re-invention, through the restless, impatient, continuing, hopeful inquiry human beings pursue in the world, with the world, and with each other" (p. 53). The specific actions individuals take may not be predictable, but for a media-literate person, they will reflect one's growing knowledge and awareness, along with the insights from engaging in media analysis, evaluation, and creation.

It's important to note here that for some educators—and perhaps for many parents—a primary goal of media literacy is to protect children (and society) from the potentially harmful effects of media. In that paradigm, the outcomes (actions) might well focus on limiting time and exposure to certain types of media and media content or making healthy choices that are often described in terms of morality (e.g., good versus bad snack foods). In school-based media literacy education, however, the primary goal is not protection but rather the development of knowledge, skills, and empowerment. Rather than protecting children and teens from "bad" media, the goal should be to develop media-literate students who are better at identifying misinformation and disinformation, more likely to recognize and challenge stereotypes, less likely to fall for misleading nutritional claims, and less prone to imitating media violence or engaging in cyberbullying. But protection is not the main goal. As Scheibe and Rogow (2012) have noted, we don't teach children to read in order to protect them from harmful books; rather, reading is an essential skill that will empower them their whole lives. The same is true for media literacy education.

What Is Critical Thinking?

When Cyndy asks her college students, "How many of you have been told you should engage in critical thinking?" almost every student raises a hand. When she then asks, "What does that mean—*critical thinking*?" they look puzzled. No one had really explained what they were expected to do to be a critical thinker. In their book *The Teacher's Guide to Media Literacy* (2012), Cyndy and her coauthor, Faith Rogow, identified these components of critical thinking:

- **Being in the game of asking questions**—having the desire to question, to know things and know about things; being in the habit of asking questions
- **Being inherently skeptical**—not accepting statements at face value, but instead being ready to question the validity of statements, looking for evidence as to the motives and assumptions behind stated claims
- **Valuing logical reasoning**—being able to distinguish between facts and opinion; acknowledging that facts have to matter and the conclusions have to be logically grounded in evidence
- **Being flexible and open-minded**—being aware of and questioning our own biases and assumptions; being willing to change our minds in light of new evidence

In *Asking the Right Questions,* Browne and Keeley (2014) describe the values of a critical thinker in similar terms, saying that a critical thinker has *curiosity, humility, autonomy,* and *respect for good reasoning.* They also differentiate between "weak sense critical thinking"—questioning claims and messages that you disagree with or that come from a source that you distrust—and "strong sense critical thinking," which includes being ready to apply the same skepticism and questions to messages from sources you typically do trust and that fit with your own assumptions and beliefs. This notion of weak sense and strong sense doesn't mean that we should *always* question or distrust *everything* we see, read, and hear—doing so often leads to cynicism—but we should be ready to question without being resistant or defensive. It also means that we shouldn't automatically trust messages from certain sources and automatically distrust messages from other sources, and that although we may look to fact checkers (such as snopes .com or factcheck.org) for information and insights, we shouldn't automatically rely on their judgments in place of our own. We need to be ready to do the heavy lifting of critical thinking ourselves.

Integrating Media Literacy and Critical Thinking in the K–12 Classroom

In 2007, the National Association for Media Literacy Education (NAMLE) published the *Core Principles of Media Literacy Education in the United States,* which opened with this statement:

> The purpose of media literacy education is to help individuals of all ages develop the habits of inquiry and skills of expression that they need to be critical thinkers, effective communicators and active citizens in today's world. (Bergsma et al., p. 1)

The authors go on to emphasize that, as with print literacy, media literacy education should be designed to build upon and reinforce skills at all developmental levels, with integrated, interactive, and repeated practice. In other words, media literacy shouldn't be viewed as something to explore in a single class, during a weeklong intervention, or at only one grade level. Instead, media literacy can and should be integrated across the curriculum, in a developmental sequence that builds skills and knowledge over time. They conclude that implementing the ongoing practice of media literacy in K–12 education will lead to informed, reflective, and engaged students equipped for authentic participation in a democratic society.

This approach illustrates the importance of integrating media literacy as a methodology rather than as a single content area. And although media literacy can be taught as a specific subject, we believe that a curriculum-driven approach in which media literacy is used to teach core content and skills across disciplines and grade levels is necessary to develop habits of thinking about all media messages. As we described in Chapter 1, media literacy can be integrated into the teaching of forms of matter in a 1st grade science class. It can be easily incorporated into English language arts (e.g., in the teaching of poetry), social studies (e.g., discussing the history of presidential campaigns), math (e.g., presenting data in graphs and charts), and any other content area. In this way, media literacy doesn't become another add-on that teachers need to find a way to fit into their already overpacked curriculum. Instead, it is woven into their lessons in logical ways that engage students with many different backgrounds and abilities.

As we describe throughout the remainder of this book, media literacy can be implemented through little tweaks to existing lessons, ongoing threads throughout the school year, or through project-based learning that might incorporate extensive media analysis into the creation of media productions. The key lies in the inquiry-based process, encouraging students to be active participants in their media world—whether in the classroom or their personal lives—continually noticing and sharing their interpretations of media messages that they see, read, and hear. In this way, media literacy education is much more about teaching students *how to think*, not *what to think*.

This shift from emphasizing the teaching of facts to a focus on teaching students to inquire, problem-solve, create, and think critically is reflected in the revised educational standards in many subject areas. We recently analyzed the alignment between media literacy education and national standards for English language arts, social studies, science, math, library studies, technology, early childhood education, and journalism. We identified the following key overlapping goals:

- Student engagement in *analysis* and *evaluation* was highlighted in all eight disciplines.

- Although some emphasized specific aspects of *critical thinking* (e.g., *evidence-based analysis* for social studies and *logical thinking* in science), all disciplines included multiple references to teaching the skills and habits of *evaluation* and *analysis* throughout the curriculum.
- The same was true for *inquiry, questioning,* or *curiosity,* with some disciplines highlighting specific questioning skills and processes.
- Having students actively involved in *creation, expression,* or *communication* appeared in the standards for all eight disciplines, some with explicit reference to *media production.*

The rising importance of critical thinking, questioning, and creation in all disciplinary standards provides a key leverage point for integrating media literacy throughout the curriculum. Mediated messages have become the dominant form of communication for all ideas, be they mathematical, literary, scientific, artistic, political, or technological. Mediated messages—whether they are print, digital, graphically represented, visuals, or sound—have become essential modes of expression for all ages and in all disciplines. Critical and metacognitive reflections on these messages, both those in mass media and our own contributions, are now an essential component of literacy for all subject areas. Therefore, our charge is to figure out how to realistically include the analysis, evaluation, questioning, and creation of media messages into our already jam-packed curricula.

Key Concepts of Media Analysis

In the past four decades, every major organization involved with media literacy has identified a set of concepts about the nature of media messages that are important to keep in mind when engaging in media analysis. Although specific wording varies, there is broad agreement on six main points, which come from the *Core Principles of Media Literacy Education* developed by the National Association for Media Literacy Education (Bergsma et al., 2007). In discussing these points, we'll use the example shown in Figure 2.2—the famous painting *Discovery of the Mississippi,* created by American artist William H. Powell in 1855—to explore how each concept relates to the analysis of media messages. We'll be coming back to this painting in later chapters as we discuss how to lead a constructivist media decoding activity with students. The paragraphs following Figure 2.2 describe the six points developed by NAMLE.

FIGURE 2.2 *Discovery of the Mississippi* Painting

Source: Library of Congress. Public domain.

1. All media messages are "constructed." Every media message is constructed in some way—sometimes casually, sometimes with great attention to detail, and almost always with particular goals in mind. In doing media analysis, it's always important to consider how the message was crafted and by whom. That consideration is the difference between simply using media in the classroom (to present information, to get students engaged in a topic, etc.) and engaging in media literacy. *Discovery of the Mississippi* is carefully designed to focus attention on Hernando de

Soto, the leader of the Spanish explorers, by putting him in the center on a white horse, with clear space above and in front of him, and giving the impression that everyone (including the horse) is looking at or following him.

2. Each medium has different characteristics, strengths, and a unique "language" of construction. Every type of media has its own set of "grammatical" rules and techniques. Media analysis involves recognizing how those rules are applied to create different messages and impressions, including knowledge about specific vocabulary terms and common techniques used within that medium. In printed text, the grammar and concepts are familiar: nouns, verbs, sentences, paragraphs, past tense, first-person point of view, and so on. In visual texts, the grammar includes elements such as angles, lighting, juxtaposition, and movement. The "language" of audio messages includes sound effects, voiceovers, and music (including specific instruments, pitch, and rhythm). The internet has its own unique grammar that is necessary to understand, including URLs, extensions, banners, and hotlinks.

In paintings such as *Discovery of the Mississippi*, we would want to expand on the concepts for visual texts to include style, color, and brush techniques. In viewing this historical event as represented in a painting, we need to consider how the information and impressions are conveyed and how the same event might have been conveyed differently if we were reading several paragraphs about it or watching a scene from a documentary film. Which media format would be most effective in conveying the facts (or emotions) of the event, and why? What are the advantages and disadvantages of using a painting to record this moment in history? Considering the strengths and weaknesses of particular media forms is key to the analysis, evaluation, and creation of media messages, especially when considering the huge number of choices of different media formats we have today.

3. Media messages are produced for particular purposes. We often talk about mass media messages in terms of three major goals: to inform, to entertain, to persuade. Most mass media messages are created by whole teams of people, and those individuals often have other goals (e.g., to express individuality, creativity, or an opinion). A key issue to consider when analyzing the purposes behind mass media messages lies in economics—making money—so it's often important to follow the money and look at who paid for this message to be made and what they are expecting to get out of it. For example, *Discovery of the Mississippi* was commissioned by the U.S. Congress in 1847 during the era of manifest destiny. It is one of eight paintings hanging in the Rotunda of the U.S. Capitol in Washington, D.C., illustrating the history of the United States. Knowing this fact can certainly influence one's view about it, which could include seeing it as a piece of propaganda to justify or even celebrate the taking over of Native American lands.

4. All media messages contain embedded values and points of view. Media messages reflect the experiences and assumptions of producers and audiences, as well as cultural preoccupations, worldviews, and media conventions. In the painting *Discovery of the Mississippi*, for example, the fact that de Soto is depicted as the "hero" of the story (in the center of the picture, on a white horse, leading his men) reinforces a particular worldview that elevates White explorers and minimizes the importance of Native Peoples. In Chapter 3, we will spend more time deconstructing the messages in this painting in comparison to another one with a very different point of view about first contact between European explorers and Native Peoples.

5. People use their individual skills, beliefs, and experiences to construct their own meanings from media messages. Audiences are active participants when interpreting the meaning of media messages, so different people may interpret the same message differently. There are often dominant readings (that is, interpretations on which most people would agree), and there can be idiosyncratic interpretations that might not be supported by evidence in the media document or by factual information related to it (which some people know and others may not). But it is also quite possible for two people to interpret the same media text differently *without either of them being wrong*. This point is especially important for constructivist media decoding, where there is rarely one right answer and the depth of the collective analysis from different cultural perspectives is at the core of critical thinking and appreciation of cultural heritage.

When Cyndy showed this painting to a graduate student from Vietnam and asked which person she thought might be the famous explorer Hernando de Soto, the student pointed to the man raising his hat in the air near the back of the group of soldiers. Her second choice was the man underneath the flags who looked like he was praying. When eventually told that de Soto was the figure in the middle, she was astonished. "How could he be the leader? He's on a *white* horse! He's wearing jewelry and feathers! He's in the front of the other soldiers!" The follow-up conversation highlighted cultural differences between Vietnamese and European perspectives (e.g., that the color white is associated with death in certain Asian cultures, whereas it represents purity, innocence, and virtue in many European and Western cultures). This question-based analysis of rich media texts allows students to communicate their perspectives—often reflecting their identities of culture, race, ethnicity, religion, nationality, geography, gender, and so on.

6. Media and media messages can influence beliefs, attitudes, values, behaviors, and the democratic process. Being aware of the potential influences of media messages is an important goal of media literacy, and part of the media decoding process involves speculating on what those influences might be. As new types of media become ever more ubiquitous in modern society, they take on an oversized role in shaping our views of reality.

In Chapter 1, we explored how changes in media technology and economics influenced who voters chose for president. This is just one example of the impact media have on society, culture, and politics. In the case of the painting *Discovery of the Mississippi*, which has been viewed by millions of visitors to the U.S. Capitol, one could certainly speculate on the influence it might have on beliefs about that event (including erroneous ones), as well as stereotypes about Native Peoples. The racist impact of this worldview, intended or not, has been multigenerational. The work, paid for by the U.S. federal government, was reproduced in many elementary school history textbooks, often with limited description and certainly no critical questions. We think it likely that many students—particularly visual learners—learned more history from that "illustration" than from the printed words that surrounded it in the textbook. Through a guided constructivist media decoding and reflective discussion, students can begin to see how the painting both reflected and perpetuated Eurocentric views of settlement, Native Peoples, and U.S. history.

This book focuses on how to lead students through the process of analyzing media messages in order to unpack concepts such as those just described. The particular inquiry-based approach requires active roles for both the students and the teacher in a dialectical process designed to deconstruct the messages while collectively constructing shared meaning. This is what we call *constructivist media decoding*.

GETTING STARTED: THE BASICS OF CMD

Quite simply, constructivist media decoding is a specific way of leading students through an analysis of a media document (video clip, social media post, advertisement, song, etc.) by asking questions and probing students for evidence and elaboration. It is grounded in inquiry-based learning and teaching with the goals of collaborative engagement and joint understanding. During a CMD activity, the teacher leads students through a critical "reading" of diverse media "texts," applying knowledge to interpret and evaluate the messages they see, read, or hear. As we'll describe in Chapter 4, this approach to media decoding can be done individually or in pairs, in the classroom or as a homework assignment, led by the teacher or led by students. But for now, we'll focus on doing CMD as a whole-class activity led by the teacher in the classroom (or online using a synchronous approach).

One easy way to get started doing CMD activities with your class is by using one or more of the free lessons created by Project Look Sharp that are appropriate for your grade level and subject area (available at https://projectlooksharp.org/lessons). Grounded in relevant learning standards and media literacy goals, these activities typically use the CMD process to teach core content as well as media literacy skills. They can also serve as a model as you begin to develop your own CMD activities with media examples that will work for your goals and educational context.

In this chapter and the next, we'll lay out practical steps for getting started in leading your own CMD activities, with tips and cautions to keep in mind as you build this work into your teaching practice. But first, let's dig a little deeper into what we mean by "constructivist" media decoding.

What Do We Mean by "Constructivist"?

The idea of constructivism stems from the developmental theories of Jean Piaget and Lev Vygotsky, both of whom argued that children gradually develop an understanding of the world through their interactions with it. Piaget laid out four stages of cognitive development from infancy through adolescence. These stages describe predictable qualitative changes in children's reasoning abilities, which he called "schemes"—ways of knowing or acting on the world. Although Piaget tended to focus on children's understanding of the physical world through exploration and interaction with objects, his emphasis on active construction of knowledge has had a strong influence on education and the importance of providing rich and varied experiences for children's active learning (Scheibe, 2018).

Lev Vygotsky's social constructivist (or sociocultural) theory is similar to Piaget's in its emphasis on active learning and construction of understanding. Unlike Piaget, however, Vygotsky emphasizes how other people (parents, teachers, older and more skilled peers) can help children learn through dialogue (including explanation, demonstration, and feedback on performance). Rather than simply focusing on children's current level of demonstrated knowledge and skills, Vygotsky argued for the importance of children's *zone of proximal development:* the range of capability reflecting what children are capable of doing by themselves and what they are capable of doing with the assistance of another person. His concept of *scaffolding*—in which parents and teachers provide the environment, structure, and hints to foster powerful learning rather than telling the child directly what to do—is strongly reflected in the CMD process.

Teachers and learners are engaged in a continuous process of articulating their own views and perspectives in order to negotiate shared meaning (Kozulin, Gindis, Ageyev, & Miller, 2003).

In media literacy education, teachers regularly scaffold media analysis by providing questions and follow-up probes, building the students' skills in analysis and evaluation so that they can eventually ask their own questions about media messages and reflect on their—and others'—interpretations of them. By engaging in media analysis as a collective process—in which students can hear the interpretations of their peers—the focus is on unpacking the students' own analysis while probing for evidence to back up their statements. This approach is central to the CMD process: it is not about the teacher helping students see the "true" meaning in the media document, or even moving the entire class to a single, agreed-upon interpretation. Instead, the students and teacher learn from each other—and each time, the conversation and conclusions are likely to be a little different. This process also encourages self-reflection about one's own interpretations and biases, leading to a deeper understanding of both the media messages and one's self (an outcome for both the students and the teacher).

CMD as an Inquiry-Based Literacy Process

As we explained in Chapter 2, media literacy is an extension of traditional literacy (reading and writing), applied to all of the different forms of media through which we get information, impressions, and ideas. CMD is grounded in this deep collective "reading" of media messages that parallels many aspects of information literacy and visual literacy. It can be applied to virtually any topic and curriculum area and therefore overlaps with scientific literacy, quantitative literacy, health literacy, cultural literacy, and other forms of literacy that each reflect different content areas.

As with all literacy education, media literacy involves the development of skills through repeated practice. It often involves applying knowledge (from prior experience, from last night's homework, etc.) to the process of analyzing and evaluating a media document. And when integrated throughout a curriculum—especially in a developmental sequence from early childhood through high school—it results in increasing sophistication in the "deep reading" of print and visual texts, coupled with "deep listening" for the audio elements of the message (including music, voiceovers, and sound effects).

Applying media literacy analysis to information sources involves going beyond the content and information to be gained from the source, or even learning about the author and illustrator and their credentials. It's about taking a deep look at the nature of the media source itself, looking "behind the curtain" to explore how the media document was constructed and why, to evaluate how its credibility might be perceived by different audiences, and to view it in the broader context of culture and worldview. If the media example is a textbook, for example, we might examine the cover and discuss the messages conveyed by it, how it reflects the content of the book (or strays from it), and what purposes it might serve for the publisher. We might examine the table of contents to see what is included and what is left out, speculating on why that might be the case, given the time period and goals of the author. We might well explore the illustrations in the book with the same intensity that we read the text, discussing the impressions conveyed by the photographs, paintings, and diagrams, noting the extent to which they add to—or distract from—the textual content. We might compare two or more textbooks on the same topic from different time periods or aimed at different audiences, reflecting on how those differences might influence what we learn about the topic.

The practice of comparing two media examples that represent different perspectives is a common one in media literacy education and can be an easy way to get started doing constructivist media decoding with students. For example, look at the two excerpts from different encyclopedia entries about Islam shown in Figure 3.1. One is taken from *Encyclopedia Britannica Online;* the other is from Islam.com, a website created from an Islamic perspective. Take a few minutes to read these two entries, then decide which one is from *Encyclopedia Britannica Online* and which one is from Islam.com. What's your evidence to support your conclusions? What similarities and what differences can you identify? Is one entry more credible than the other? What makes you say that? And would everyone agree?

FIGURE 3.1 **Definitions of Islam**	
Islam: Major world religion founded by Muhammad in Arabia in the early 7th century AD. The Arabic word Islam means "submission"—specifically, submission to the will of the one God, called Allah in Arabic. Islam is a strictly monotheistic religion, and its adherents, called Muslims, regard the Prophet Muhammad as the last and most perfect of God's messengers, who include Adam, Abraham, Moses, Jesus, and others.	**Islam:** The literal meaning of Islam is peace; surrender of one's will, i.e., losing oneself for the sake of God and surrendering one's own pleasure for the pleasure of God. The message of Islam was revealed to the Holy Prophet Muhammad (peace and blessings on him) 1,400 years ago. It was revealed through the angel Gabriel (on whom be peace) and was thus preserved in the Holy Quran.

Which is from **Islam.com** and which is from **Britannica.com**? Give your **evidence** from the text!

Source: © 2005 Project Look Sharp. Used with permission.

You've just done a constructivist media decoding—guided by specific questions that ask you to analyze the messages you saw and to give evidence to support your impressions and conclusions. It is an approach that can be easily applied to just about any piece of media and is designed to build those habits of inquiry along with fundamental literacy skills that will engage and empower students in both school and their personal lives. It is worth noting that although most media documents used for decoding activities ask students to apply prior knowledge, this example of a decoding activity uses media documents to actually *teach* core subject knowledge while also providing practice in critical thinking.

Focusing on Questions

CMD strongly reflects the broad approach to education known as *inquiry-based learning,* with most of the emphasis on asking questions rather than providing information. There may be some context or background information that will be important for students to know ahead of time (or to be given during the decoding process), but the bulk of what the teacher says during the decoding activity should come in the form of questions and probes for evidence and understanding.

Many of the questions will reflect specific content goals for that particular subject area—such as the questions about different types of matter that were asked of the 1st graders watching *Spider-Man vs. Hydro-Man,* described in Chapter 1, or questions about Islam in the example just presented. Developing an ongoing practice of inquiry-based learning through the incorporation of CMD activities can start by taking statements made during a typical lecture designed to communicate information and ideas and flipping them to become questions about what the students are reading, seeing, or hearing. Content-based questions can start broadly ("What do you notice about this bar graph?"), or they might be very specific ("What were the messages about anthropogenic CO_2 in that short film?"). The key is to follow up with probing questions designed to get students to give evidence to back up their responses ("What makes you say that?" or "Where did you see that in the film?").

CMD activities are also likely to include media literacy questions such as those shown in Figure 3.2. These key questions for analyzing media messages, which are adapted from many previous versions developed by media literacy organizations across the world, are available as both handouts and wall posters on the Project Look Sharp website (https://project looksharp.org/handouts).

FIGURE 3.2 **Key Questions to Ask When Analyzing Media Messages**

AUTHORSHIP

Who made this?

PURPOSES

Why was this made?
Who is their target audience?
What do they want me to do?
What do they want me to think (or think about)?

CONTENT

What are the messages about _____?
What ideas, values, and information are overt? Implied?
What is left out that might be important to know?
How does this compare/contrast to other media messages on this topic?

TECHNIQUES

What techniques are used to communicate the messages?
How effective are those techniques? What are their strengths and weaknesses?
Why might they have chosen to use those techniques?

CONTEXT

When was this created?
Where and how was it shared with the public?
What aspects of cultural context are relevant to consider?
How does this amplify or counteract existing patterns (on the topic, by the author, etc.)?
How does the media form (social media, print, TV, etc.) impact the message?

ECONOMICS

Who paid for this?
Who might make money from this?

CREDIBILITY

Is this fact, opinion, or something else?
How credible is the information?
What are the sources of the ideas or assertions?
Is this a trustworthy source about this particular topic?

EFFECTS

Who might benefit from this message?
Who might be harmed by it?
Whose voices are represented or privileged?
Whose voices are omitted or silenced?

INTERPRETATIONS

What is my interpretation of this?
How do prior experiences and beliefs shape my interpretation?
What do I learn about myself from my interpretation or reaction?
How (and why) might different people interpret this differently?

RESPONSES

How does this make me feel?
What kinds of actions might I take in response to this?

And . . .
What's my evidence?
Why might that matter?
Why do I think that?
What else do I want (or need) to know?
How could I find that out?

Source: Created by Cyndy Scheibe and Chris Sperry, Project Look Sharp, and Faith Rogow, Insighters Educational Consulting. Creative Commons license.

Pause to Reflect

Take some time to look over the categories and questions shown in Figure 3.2. In the context of your own teaching—keeping in mind your curriculum area(s) and grade level(s)—which questions do you think are most important for your students to be in the habit of asking, and why? What questions are you already using in your work with students, and which ones might you consider asking in the future?

When using these key questions with students, it's important to focus more on the *categories* of questions than on the specific wording; the handout is intended as a guide rather than a script. Considering *authorship* and *purpose* is often a powerful way to get at bias and perspective, but you might ask about it differently with a high school student ("How might the goals of the writer be different from those of the publisher?") than you would with a child in kindergarten ("What do they want you to do?").

Notice that although many of the key questions focus on the construction and content of the media message itself, some focus on the impact of the message on those who see, read, or hear it. These include powerful questions about the potential benefits and harm to different audiences, a topic that we explore more fully in Chapter 5. They also include meta-cognitive questions about one's own feelings and responses to the media message, which is core to unpacking things such as *confirmation bias* in relation to news media. Although some of these issues might be challenging to explore with younger children, a developmentally appropriate CMD activity can begin to raise questions about these concepts ("What might happen if someone thought that SunnyD and Froot Loops actually had a lot of fruit in them?" "Why do you think the toymakers might try to pretend that these little cars are bigger than they really are?").

Also notice the follow-up probe questions at the bottom of the key questions document (in the "And" section). As we've mentioned before, those probes are core to the CMD process. They often push students to articulate their thinking and provide scaffolding for many types of assessments that are used in secondary grades ("Give evidence to back up your conclusions"). Probe questions can also be used to expand on the discussion ("Tell me more about that"), to clarify statements ("Can you explain a little more about what you mean?"), and to encourage multiple interpretations ("Does everyone agree?" "Do you think anybody might feel differently about this message?").

Finally, you certainly wouldn't ask all of these questions, no matter how much time you have for a decoding, nor do you need to ask them in this particular order. For both content-based and media literacy questions, you'll want to pick and choose to find a small number of questions that will be appropriate for your grade level and curriculum area and that will get you where you want to go with this activity. We'll talk more about the art of asking CMD questions in Chapter 4, but identifying your goals for the decoding—focusing on where you want to get to—is always an important part of the CMD process.

Aligning with Your Goals

As you begin to think about designing and leading a CMD with your students, it's often helpful to start by thinking about your goals. These are likely to include both *content-related goals* (the information or concepts you want students to understand) and *media literacy/critical-thinking goals* (analyzing and evaluating media messages and their effects). Some of those goals may reflect learning standards that you need to address in a particular lesson, or that emerge from a reading, from homework, or from earlier classwork. You may have other goals as well, such as encouraging participation by all students (including those who rarely raise their hands) or engaging students in a challenging conversation about cultural or gender stereotypes. Being clear about your goals in doing a given CMD is an important first step.

Consider the story described in Chapter 1 about the 1st grade teacher's goals for teaching her students about the qualities of liquid matter. That goal led the librarian she was working with to creatively search for examples from popular media that reflected different forms of matter and that would be engaging for 5- and 6-year-old children. Some of the questions that the teacher asked the children about the *Spider-Man vs. Hydro-Man* cartoon were designed to address those goals. Others reflected media literacy goals, including questions about why the cartoon maker would show something that couldn't really happen, and it was those questions that really demonstrated the children's potential to engage in deep thinking about the constructed nature of cartoons.

Here's another example from a lesson posted on the Project Look Sharp website that is based on the famous painting *Discovery of the Mississippi* that we described in Chapter 2 to illustrate key concepts of media analysis. At Project Look Sharp, we used that painting, coupled with another painting by a different artist from a different time period, as the basis for a social studies lesson we designed in collaboration with 4th grade teachers in our local school district. The teachers had four goals in mind for their students:

1. Learning about first contact between European explorers and Native Peoples during the period of westward expansion across the United States
2. Understanding cultural perspectives and points of view
3. Developing conclusions and providing evidence from the document to back them up
4. Working effectively to engage all students in the class

After meeting with the teachers to discuss their goals, we found the pair of paintings shown in Figure 3.3 for the students to decode. We developed a lesson plan and guide for the teachers to lead their 4th grade students through a decoding of *Discovery of the Mississippi* first, followed by a comparison decoding of *The Last Supper*.

FIGURE 3.3 *Discovery of the Mississippi* and *The Last Supper* Paintings

Discovery of the Mississippi, William Powell, 1855

The Last Supper, Jonathan Warm Day, 1991

Source: Discovery of the Mississippi, Library of Congress. Public domain.
The Last Supper, © Jonathan Warm Day. Reproduced with permission.

Given the teachers' goals for this activity, we wanted them to be able to ask challenging questions about the different perspectives of first contact between European explorers and Native Peoples in these two paintings, and to explore the messages about those two groups of people in each painting. But it's often helpful to start with some simpler questions that anyone can answer—particularly if you have a pretty good idea what the answers are likely to be. In this case, showing only the first painting, we started with a brief statement about it: "This is a painting that portrays the famous Spanish explorer Hernando de Soto. Which one do you think is de Soto?" This question always leads to laughter and many raised hands, identifying de Soto as "the guy on the white horse" or "the guy in the middle." In a CMD, you would want to follow immediately with a probe question—"What makes you say *he* is de Soto?"—and to get answers from several students.

After that, the conversation has the potential to go in many different directions, so it's important for teachers to keep their goals in mind, guiding the conversation back with new questions that balance ease of response (to engage all students) with an increasing focus on the messages conveyed in the painting about first contact. These questions might include the following:

- "What adjective would you use to describe de Soto, based on how he is shown in the painting?"
- "What are the messages about the European explorers in this painting?"
- "According to the painting, how might the Native People feel about de Soto and his men?"
- "Whose perspective or point of view does this painting portray?"

That last question is an important one to end with—and then to *start* with after introducing the second painting as another representation of first contact. Depending on the time available, the decoding might include showing both paintings side by side to identify similarities and differences in messages, artistic techniques, and impressions. You might also introduce the titles and artists for each painting—*Discovery of the Mississippi* by American artist William Powell, and *The Last Supper* by Taos Pueblo artist Jonathan Warm Day—to discuss the implications of each title in the context of the perspective of each artist, including the bias inherent in describing the arrival of European explorers as a "discovery."

This lesson (which is featured on the Project Look Sharp website) was effective in meeting the goals the teachers had laid out, including engaging *all* students, and not just those typically "good" students who always raised their hands. Like many media documents, paintings like these can be used in different ways at different grade levels and in different curriculum areas—and we'll come back to these paintings in Chapter 4 to illustrate that point.

Using CMD with Diverse Types of Media Examples

In Chapter 2, we talked about "media" encompassing a huge range of formats—from books to social media, from paintings to TV commercials. As you begin to use CMD with your students, work to apply it to as many different media types as possible. One reason for this practice is to enable students to ask questions about all sorts of different types of media examples and not get stuck in thinking that CMD applies only to certain types of media, such as news or advertising.

CMD can be used with short, print-based texts, as well as nearly any audio, visual, or audiovisual media example. Audio and audiovisual examples are important to decode in order to develop listening skills, including listening to background music and sound effects that are often used to convey different emotions or to highlight the importance of a particular action. It's also critical to lead CMDs with websites and other digital media, including those that students are typically using in their everyday lives. Developing habits of inquiry, analysis, and evaluation has never been more important, especially around issues of credibility, bias, and manipulation.

It's also important to do CMD with both academic/educational media and contemporary/entertainment media. A CMD activity sometimes starts with an engaging media example that the teacher finds or comes across (e.g., seen in a tweet, found on a cereal box, arriving in a piece of direct mail). It may also come from media examples found in the classroom that are used to convey information but have never been analyzed in the context of media literacy, with questions about authorship, techniques of construction, and so on. You can repurpose media that you already use regularly in the classroom for this type of analysis by simply adding one or two questions (with probes) as part of your regular lesson.

A high school biology teacher we worked with told us about a film about oil spills that she had regularly shown to her students without ever thinking about who had made it: Exxon. When she shared this information with her students and asked them to look for any indications of bias in favor of oil companies that might show up in the film because of who made it, she was astonished to find that students were paying much more attention to the film and could pick out several subtle but clear examples.

You may also find that you can apply course concepts to unexpected media forms. English language arts lessons designed to teach literary elements, for example, have traditionally focused on plays, novels, and short stories; but literary elements can also be identified in story narratives found in TV commercials, movie trailers, song lyrics, and paintings (such as those shown in Figure 3.3). Elementary teachers have introduced math concepts by having students look for information about the number of grams of sugar on cereal packages and the percentage of juice in "fruit" drinks and flavored beverages; secondary math teachers have asked students to calculate the percentage of advertising content in newspapers and magazines versus television programs and to compare statistical results from political polls. Science principles can be used to assess the credibility of advertising claims, especially medical and nutritional claims. Students in global studies courses can analyze messages about power and values by examining money from different countries (including the United States, whose currency to date still features only White men and the phrase "In God We Trust," which was added to both paper currency and coins in the 1950s to distinguish the United States from Communist countries).

When you are first starting to do CMD activities in your work with students, you might find it easier to use some existing media literacy lessons, such as those found on the Project Look Sharp website. There are also wonderful databases that you are probably familiar with, such as the Library of Congress or *Britannica Online*, with many examples that lend themselves to constructivist decoding. And, of course, school librarians will be a terrific resource for all sorts of media materials.

Less Is More—Although Sometimes Two Is Better Than One

Although the CMD approach can theoretically be applied to entire novels or films, it's much better to apply it to short sections of text or video segments. Movie trailers, music videos, and 30-second TV commercials often work wonderfully well to explore carefully designed storylines and characters—with the advantage of being able to show those short video clips multiple times to develop a "deeper reading" each time. Showing older films and commercials allows for a discussion about historical context as well. Newspaper headlines and photo captions can provide rich opportunities for the analysis of grammar, vocabulary, and tone—and in much less time than it takes to analyze longer text-based passages.

In the same way, it is usually better to do a deep reading of a small number of media examples than to ask only one or two questions about many examples. We once worked with a gifted educator who opposed the use of tobacco and had extensive experience leading decodings of tobacco advertisements with middle school students. She demonstrated her approach for us, moving through 20 to 30 ads in less than half an hour. After participating in our weeklong summer institute and seeing the power of doing deep readings of media examples, she said she realized she needed to change her approach radically to do much deeper decodings of only three or four advertisements in the same amount of time. That depth of analysis—especially coupled with ongoing probing for evidence and clarification—is what leads to higher-order thinking, along with more skilled observation and listening skills.

On the other hand, doing a comparison of two (or more) media documents—such as the examples shown in Figures 3.1 and 3.3 earlier in this chapter—is a particularly powerful way to do a CMD activity, lending itself easily to compare-and-contrast skill building. You can also show a set of images and ask students to identify patterns. For instance, using front pages from newspapers all over the world obtained from www.freedomforum .org/todaysfrontpages/#1, a Spanish-language class could look at English- and Spanish-language newspaper headlines and images from the same day to develop language skills, while also applying media literacy skills to identify differences in the ways U.S. and Latin American press present the news about a current event. This type of compare-and-contrast activity can even be done with younger children—for example, by analyzing the messages on boxes of various children's cereals. We'll see more examples of comparison CMDs in later chapters.

Getting Started with a CMD Activity Plan

By now, you have a pretty good sense of how the CMD process works, and you might already have ideas about how to begin using it in your own teaching context. When we do professional development work with teachers, after laying out the basics of CMD with lots of demonstrations and "noticings" about how the process works, we ask the participants to pick one idea to flesh out in a simple CMD activity plan. As the example in Figure 3.4 shows, this plan has six elements:

1. Providing information about the *teaching context* for the activity
2. Identifying a few *content-based and media literacy/critical-thinking objectives*
3. Identifying one or two *media examples* for analysis
4. Identifying a few *key questions (and probes)* to ask about each of the media documents
5. Developing a *decoding plan* that lays out what background information might be necessary and when to share it, the sequencing of the questions and probes, and notes about how the activity might progress
6. Identifying *pre- and post-decoding activities,* if appropriate

We've already laid out the basics for the first four elements, which can get you started. In later chapters, we'll go into more detail about how to develop a decoding plan and how to frame the CMD activities in the overall context of a lesson or curriculum.

In the next chapter, we'll explore deeper aspects of the CMD approach, including tips for integrating media decoding as part of your existing curriculum and how to do CMD using remote online technologies—as either synchronous or asynchronous activities—with your students. We'll also talk about common pitfalls that educators may experience when doing media decoding in the classroom with students, along with ways to address them, using rich examples from teaching practice in K–12 settings.

FIGURE 3.4 **CMD Activity Plan for 1st Grade Lesson on Liquid Matter**

1. Teaching Context
Grade level: 1   Subject area: Science and ELA   Unit: Matter
This activity will come near the end of our unit on matter, after students understand the qualities of liquids.

2. Objectives (i.e., CCSS for literacy, media literacy):

2a: Content-Based Objective:
Students will identify the properties of a liquid (i.e., takes the shape of the object it is in, has mass and takes up space, can turn into gas).

2b: Media Literacy/Critical-Thinking Objectives:
  • Students will ask and answer questions about a text, describe relevant details, and express ideas clearly.
  • Students will analyze the credibility of a (fiction) text, including identifying its purpose, the techniques used to communicate messages, and its scientific accuracy.

3. Media Example
This two-minute excerpt from the animated cartoon *Hydro-Man vs. Spider-Man* (15:30–17:35) shows Hydro-Man fighting with Mary Jane and Spider-Man. It shows both accurate and inaccurate qualities of liquid: accurate—has mass (hits the workers with force), takes up space (the sand covers it), turns to gas when heated (the ending shot); inaccurate—doesn't take a form of its own.

4. Key Questions
  • *From what you learned about liquids, what is accurate and inaccurate in this clip?*
  • *Why might people who made the* Spider-Man *clip have shown us inaccurate information about liquids?*

5. Decoding Plan
I intend to move from an initial focus on the science presented in the clip, helping my students to see how a cartoon can include inaccurate information and accurate scientific facts, to the literacy/critical-thinking learning about credibility and accuracy. This clip will be a great hook for my students, but I will need to show it twice—the first time to let them enjoy the action and the second time to focus on the scientific information.

Before showing the clip the second time, I will review what they know about liquid matter, probing for understanding that liquid takes the shape of the object it is in (it flows), it does have mass (it can hurt) and takes up space, and it can turn into gas (if heated).

I will ask them the following question: *Who thinks they know what hydro means?* (like *hydrant*). I will relate that to Hydro-Man.

I will then introduce the second showing by asking them to look for how the filmmakers use water: *What about water in this clip is accurate (true), and what could not happen because of the qualities of water we just reviewed?*

After the second showing, I will probe for content knowledge about liquids: *What did the water do in that clip?* (*it was a puddle, it had no shape, it moved up and made a shape, it went into a solid, it evaporated*). *What things could happen? Why?* (*force hitting workers, puddle with no shape, evaporation*). *What couldn't happen? Why?* (*solid form, shape by itself, arms changing into water*).

I will continually probe for text-based evidence when students have the right answer: *Where did you see that in the clip?*

Once students understand the science in the clip, I will move on to the media literacy questions: *Why would the makers of* Spider-Man *show something that wasn't possible?*

If necessary, I will scaffold this question: *Why do you think this cartoon was made?* (*entertainment, fun*). *Was the purpose to teach us about science?*

Finally, I will see if the students can generalize about credibility: *What does this teach you about watching TV, about what we can trust and not trust to have truthful scientific information?*

6. Pre- and Post-Decoding Activities

This activity comes near the end of our Matter unit, in which I teach about matter, including through literature (*Goldilocks*), labs, and poetry (*What's the Matter?*). NOTE: Given the gender dynamics in the class, I may want to follow up on MJ's comment in the *Hydro-Man* clip: "Mori, you don't force yourself on the people you love."

4

TIPS FOR INTEGRATING CMD INTO TEACHING AND LEARNING

As you've already seen, there are many different ways to integrate constructivist media decoding—and media literacy in general—into the curriculum. You may find yourself ready to get started but not sure if you'll be able to find a way to squeeze this element into your already overfull school day. If there's one response that we've heard more than any other during our 25 years of working with K–12 educators in all grade levels and subject areas, it is this: "Sounds great, but I don't have time!" Rest assured that regular, effective teaching of the critical-thinking skills related to media literacy does not need to be a time stressor. No matter how you approach this process, there are some common tips—and cautions—to keep in mind.

Teaching Both Content and Media Literacy

In our trainings with teachers, we talk a lot about the importance of aligning the CMD activity to their goals, their specific subject area, their grade level, and the unique group of students they are teaching. Then when we give teachers the opportunity to practice leading a CMD for us and the other teacher attendees, it often seems like they forget those considerations and lead the decoding using somewhat random questions and probes. We've learned that it's important to keep issues of alignment front and center when helping educators design a CMD activity.

As we've already discussed in the previous chapter, any media decoding activity—like all classroom activities—should be driven by your goals. It is not unusual to find a cool media document such as a video clip, a podcast excerpt, or a cartoon that you are eager to analyze with your students; but without clear goals for doing that decoding, the conversation may just ramble or devolve into competing viewpoints about the meaning of the media message. The important work of Grant Wiggins and Jay McTighe (2005) in their seminal book *Understanding by Design* teaches us the methodology of backward design—moving from our goals, to our assessments, to our instructional strategies. The choice of media examples and questions, therefore, should reflect your objectives for the activity, while the broader lessons and units should reflect your sequential plan for facilitating the growth of your students' learning.

When designing a CMD activity, consider incorporating both subject-area objectives and media literacy objectives (along with any goals you may have regarding group interactions such as respectful listening). This consideration is important for a number of reasons. First, if you are going to find the time and space in your overburdened curriculum to teach these types of media literacy skills, you need to use media decoding as a platform for simultaneously teaching core subject-area knowledge and concepts. Second, developing habits of inquiry in different contexts across a wide range of media examples will foster media analysis and critical thinking as habits that can be applied to any subject area inside school, and to the students' lives outside school as well.

So, although many people may perceive media decoding as primarily about teaching media literacy, we would argue that it is equally important to design media decoding activities with clear subject-area objectives in mind—including knowledge-based objectives that are specifically aligned to grade-level state learning standards. Media decoding activities can be terrific opportunities for students to practice using the vocabulary and applying the information you have been teaching, as well as providing a platform for introducing new knowledge through content-rich media documents such as video clips, websites, and articles. You can also introduce new subject-area knowledge, vocabulary, and concepts through the background information presented before the decoding and through additional information that you share throughout the analysis.

However, although the subject knowledge and concept-driven objectives are key components of most CMD activities, to be a media literacy activity, the lesson must also include critical analysis of the constructed nature of media messages. Teachers from content-heavy disciplines like social studies and science are typically comfortable using diverse media to teach and reinforce key information, but they often miss the opportunity to integrate media literacy and critical thinking into their lessons.

Unlike the traditional uses of media in the classroom to illustrate, inform, engage, and perhaps entertain, media decoding scrutinizes the media document itself. Figure 4.1 illustrates the types of media literacy objectives that can be integrated into CMD activities, often by simply adding a question or probing for evidence to back up a content-based response. You might consider posting a copy of these objectives (and the key questions for analyzing media messages that were introduced in Chapter 3, Figure 3.2, p. 44) above the computer where you design your lessons. Whenever you show a video clip, introduce an article, go to a website, or hand out a textbook, you have the opportunity to ask one or two media literacy questions that apply to that document.

If media literacy is to be a legitimate and consistent component of your teaching, you should also have media literacy objectives built into your CMD lessons. Many of these objectives may look familiar, as they reflect some of the standards that appear in English language arts, social studies, science, health, library, and many other subject areas. Over time, your content-area objectives and media literacy objectives will become interwoven, but initially it is important to delineate each so that you are consistently integrating the objectives from both disciplines.

FIGURE 4.1 Media Literacy Objectives

Habits of Questioning
Students will...
- Cite specific textual evidence to support their analysis.
- Ask questions about authorship, techniques, credibility, etc.

Authorship, Purpose, and Target Audience
Students will...
- Analyze the source and purpose of the media message.
- Compare the points of view of two or more media sources.
- Identify any economic motivations behind a message.
- Identify what the makers want them to think about or do.
- Identify bias in media messages.
- Determine the target audience for a media message.

Content, Techniques, and Context
Students will...
- Identify the messages in media.
- Note techniques in media construction.
- Evaluate the effectiveness of the techniques used.
- Compare how different authors treat similar topics.
- Consider what is left out of a message.
- Identify which perspectives/voices are included and missing.
- Identify cultural context, when it was created, where and how it was shared, etc.
- Identify how the media form (social media, print, TV, etc.) may affect the message.

- Consider how this message amplifies or counteracts existing patterns (on the topic, by the author, etc.).

Credibility
Students will...
- Differentiate between facts and opinions.
- Identify and distinguish conflicting claims.
- Reflect on the credibility of scientific information.
- Distinguish news, opinion, and advocacy.
- Identify arguments and claims.

Responses and Impact
Students will...
- Determine who might benefit and who might be harmed by a media message.
- Determine how different people might interpret the same media message in different ways.
- Reflect on the potential impact of media messages on different people.
- Consider how one's gender, racial, or political identity influences one's interpretation.
- Reflect on how their own biases influence their interpretations and responses.
- Identify what they learn about themselves from reflecting on their interpretations and reactions.
- Notice their emotional responses to a media message.
- Identify actions they can take in response to media messages.

Source: © 2019 Project Look Sharp. Used with permission.

Finding the Right Media Documents

We've already stressed that you can do CMD activities with many different types of media examples. But not all media messages lend themselves to decoding in the classroom. It's important to start with relevant, readable, rich, and engaging media documents, ones that lend themselves to questions that you can follow up with probes for students to provide evidence for their conclusions and interpretations. You may decide to focus on a single media example for a deep "reading," or to use a pair of media examples (or an even larger set) so that the analysis can include comparisons across different viewpoints, techniques, or historical periods. You'll also need to consider the appropriateness and accessibility of media documents for your context and specific group of students.

A CMD activity sometimes starts with an engaging media example that the teacher finds or comes upon (in a news feed or on social media, for example). We urge educators to "keep their Velcro buds open"—identifying interesting things they see, read, and hear in their own media experiences as potential examples for a future media decoding. When that happens—and this seems obvious—try to save the item right away (e.g., in a folder on your desktop). We have both had many instances when we remember having seen the perfect media example to use in a lesson and then couldn't find it again despite our best attempts. We've learned to take a screenshot of an image we see online (and rename it so we'll recognize it later), to download videos and articles, and to copy the URLs from websites and YouTube into a Word document with a brief explanation. And like many educators, we're not afraid to ask if we can take a newspaper or magazine that we find at the dentist's office or the home of a friend.

More typically, CMD activities develop from a curriculum goal or activity that could be enriched through decoding relevant media examples. In that case, you'll need to start searching for documents that will fit your purpose, and doing so can take time. There are many online sources where you can find media examples to use for decoding, and your school librarian will be invaluable in helping you track down potential documents. In addition to the free media documents available on the Project Look Sharp website, you can find thousands of examples through free or subscription databases such as those available through the Library of Congress or *Britannica Online*.

This option raises the important issue of copyright. Is it OK to use copyrighted media examples for media decoding in the classroom without seeking permission or limiting your use in some way (e.g., not using more than 10 percent of the total)? Although your individual school or district may have specific guidelines governing the use of copyrighted materials in the classroom, be assured that using media examples as part of a CMD activity falls clearly under the fair use exemption to U.S. copyright law (Aufderheide & Jaszi, 2018; Hobbs, 2010a). As we described in Chapter 1, this fair use exemption is central to both education and democracy.

At Project Look Sharp, we faced this issue more than 15 years ago when we decided to publish our first media literacy curriculum kit, *Media Construction of War*. That kit was based on decoding more than 50 *Newsweek* magazine covers and photo spreads from the Vietnam War, the Gulf War of 1991, and the war in Afghanistan following the 9/11 attacks. Those covers included images of Ho Chi Minh, Saddam Hussein, Osama bin Laden, and many other officials and soldiers who were prominent during those three wars. When we contacted *Newsweek* in 2003 to get permission to use the images in our kit, they replied that we would need to (1) pay *Newsweek* $250 for each image; (2) receive written permission from each photographer; and (3) receive permission from each person featured in the photograph (Osama bin Laden, Saddam Hussein, and others). *Newsweek* was essentially saying no—and we took issue with that, given that they were framing our understanding of what happened during each of these wars. With the support of the Ithaca College administration, we decided to invoke the fair use exemption to copyright, and we continue to do that for all of the documents in our media decoding activities (Sperry & Scheibe, 2018).

One final note about finding media examples is this: you can encourage your students to bring in (or email) their own media examples for decoding and even have them lead a decoding of examples they have found. Some of our best media documents—including some that appear in Project Look Sharp's media literacy lesson activities—have come from our students. By engaging your students in this process, you'll be encouraging their habits of inquiry and providing opportunities for them to take action as a key part of the media literacy process. Cyndy always smiles when a student who graduated many years ago emails her to say, "I just saw this and thought of you! I knew you would love to decode it in your class!"

Setting Up the Context for Decoding

As you plan your CMD activity, take some time to think about how you'll introduce it. This step is especially important if you're just beginning to do media decoding with your students. They might not have had any experience doing this kind of detailed "reading" and analysis of media messages, and they might easily respond as they do in their personal media worlds (e.g., focusing on how much they like or dislike the message). Although you might not want to share everything about your goals for the activity, students may need some direction about what they might be looking (or listening) for before you start the decoding. This point is especially relevant with audio or audiovisual media examples; students may easily get caught up in the story or music and have little memory of specific content unless they are cued to look or listen for it ahead of time. In short, they need to be prepared to engage fully in the decoding process.

At the heart of any media decoding activity is the "reading" of one or more documents, so the "texts" need to be legible or audible, especially with respect to details that address your content and media literacy objectives. Think through how to make the document fully accessible to students based on the context in which they'll be experiencing it. This effort could be as simple as projecting slides on a whiteboard for the whole class to see, but only if the critical visual and text-based details are readable by all students. It could be as simple as showing a short video clip on a computer screen, but only if the visual and audio elements can be seen and heard clearly. It could be as simple as handing out a short reading, but only if all of the students can read it in the allotted amount of time. This consideration is an important issue of equity and inclusion that is especially vital when working with special education students and English language learners.

Here are some strategies for making your media documents accessible for a decoding activity:

- **Make copies of the entire document or the key components** (e.g., the transcript from a video or song) to pass out while students view or listen to the document.
- **Enlarge, highlight, or otherwise identify key details** in the document.
- **Play the audio/audiovisual media clip more than once,** asking progressively more complex questions each time, or with different students playing different roles (e.g., closing their eyes and focusing on the audio only, watching visuals for symbolism, noting vocabulary that sets the tone, etc.).
- **Have students work in pairs to prepare their analysis ahead of time** and then present during the whole-class decoding.
- **Have support teachers work with identified students** to access and analyze particular documents before the whole-class decoding.

In planning your decoding activity, you will also need to decide what background knowledge (if any) your students will need in order to appropriately respond to your decoding questions. In our PD work with teachers, we have noticed a general tendency for many teachers to provide more background knowledge than is really necessary for the decoding. CMD activities are usually more engaging and educational for students if they do the bulk of the talking, with the teacher asking questions with follow-up probes and facilitating the discussion so that as many students as possible have the opportunity to participate. The decoding will likely require some key knowledge, which may be found in the document itself, unpacked as part of the questioning process, or added into the conversation by the teacher at relevant points. If the document is particularly complex, with lots of new information, you might have the students read or watch or listen to it twice—once for its content and a second time for the critical analysis. You can also divide the class so that some students focus on the information in the document while the others focus on the critical analysis and media literacy aspects.

We've also noticed that teachers can err on the side of giving students too little background knowledge to do the decoding successfully. There may well be vocabulary terms that students need to know in order to understand the questions being asked during the CMD activity and to be able to use in their responses to the media analysis. They might need to know in what year the media message was originally created, or information about the individual or organization that created it. For the two paintings of first contact that were described in Chapter 3, the 4th graders needed to know that the painting showed the Spanish explorer Hernando de Soto in order to answer the very first question: "Which one do you think is de Soto?" But they didn't really need to know the names of the artists to answer questions about cultural perspective and point of view, because those could be drawn from the content and style of each painting.

It will become easier to determine how much information is enough as you get to know your students and their meaning making, but doing so always requires reassessment from year to year and with different texts. It is not unusual for the meaning of a document to change dramatically over time. For example, for many years, Chris had students studying the Gulf War of 1991 analyze a *Newsweek* cover that showed Saddam Hussein in a green hue. Students consistently interpreted the image as communicating that the Iraqi leader was evil, but in 2003 that interpretation changed. After watching continuous TV coverage of the Iraq War, students thought that the green hue was the result of Saddam being seen through night-vision goggles. In a similar vein, the nature of his high school students' analysis of the news media depicting the collapse of the World Trade Center on September 11, 2001, changed every year for the next 12 years, heavily reflecting the age at which they had directly experienced that traumatic event. When doing this work, it is important to always keep in mind Key Concept #5 for media analysis (discussed in Chapter 2): *People use their individual skills, beliefs, and experiences to construct their own meanings from media messages.*

Developing Effective Questions That Reflect Goals and Context

Working backward from your goals is most important when you are developing the questions to ask during the decoding. Although the constructivist approach requires you to follow your students' interpretations and meaning making (which may require shifting from your original plan for the activity), not being grounded in your goals means you have no map of where you want to go. The paradox here is to know where you want to go and simultaneously stay open to following your students' lead.

Embracing this complexity shifts the process of facilitation from a technical skill to an art form. We have seen many experienced teachers who always open a media decoding activity by asking the same general questions, such as "What do you notice?" or "How does this make you feel?" These might be good questions to ask if the document is a work of art and your goals are art appreciation or general exploration of the piece, and they are often used as part of a Visual Thinking Strategies (VTS) protocol (see www.VTShome.org for more information on this approach). But if your goal is to teach specific concepts in science, math, or history, then these questions would likely divert students from your objectives. The question "How does this make you feel?" will unearth the emotional experience of your students; "What do you notice?" may unleash a range of individual perspectives and related experiences (especially in younger students). Although we are genuinely interested in the social and emotional meaning making of our students, we can unearth those elements while simultaneously focusing on specific academic objectives through creative and targeted questioning and follow-up probes.

The same media document might be used in very different ways and with very different questions at different grade levels or subject areas. In Chapter 3, for example, we looked at a media decoding activity using William Henry Powell's 1855 painting *Discovery of the Mississippi* and compared the messages in it with a painting by Taos Pueblo artist Jonathan Warm Day depicting similar events. The goals of the 4th grade teachers who designed the activity included *understanding cultural perspectives, demonstrating knowledge about first contact, providing evidence to back up conclusions,* and *group work.* But what if this painting were decoded with high school students in an AP U.S. History class? What might your goals and questions be?

Pause to Reflect

Look at the two versions of the painting *Discovery of the Mississippi* in Figure 4.2. The one on the left (which we've shown in earlier chapters) was taken from a U.S. History textbook; the image was cropped from the original version (shown on the right), which hangs in the Rotunda of the U.S. Capitol in Washington, D.C. Take some time to think about what questions you might ask the students in your 11th grade AP U.S. History class if your goals were for them to *understand how historical context shaped—and continues to shape—people's perspectives about current and past events.*

Unlike the questions for the 4th grade class, which focused on first contact and compared cultural perspectives, the questions for the 11th grade class should be designed to help students to understand the contexts for historical and contemporary perspectives. Each question might need brief additional background information for students to be able to effectively respond with their analysis. Here are some examples:

FIGURE 4.2 **Cropped and Original Versions of *Discovery of the Mississippi***

Source: Library of Congress. Public domain.

Background information: This painting, *Discovery of the Mississippi,* was commissioned by the U.S. Congress and hangs in the Rotunda of the U.S. Capitol. It was painted by a well-known American artist, William Henry Powell, in 1855.

- "What was happening in the United States at the time this painting was made that is reflected in its depiction of history?"

Background information: This painting appears in many contemporary elementary U.S. History textbooks to illustrate first contact between Native Americans and Europeans, but the textbooks typically crop the righthand section of the painting so that the cross does not appear.

- "Why might contemporary textbook publishers crop out the cross?"
- "What might that suggest about how perspectives on history have changed over time?"

Sequencing Questions and Using Follow-up Probes

The questions just presented align with the objectives, but they are not necessarily the first questions the teacher would ask. Even at the 11th grade level, to get students to the point that they could tackle those big questions, the teacher might want to have them first explore the document more generally, through questions such as these: "What are the messages here about de Soto? About Native Peoples? About power and control? About U.S. history?" If the class has been reading about de Soto and other early explorers, the teacher might want to ask knowledge-based questions such as "Who was de Soto, and what was he 'discovering'?" In addition, the teacher should have the students probe for evidence in the document that backs up significant interpretations by asking, "What makes you say that?" or "Where or how is that portrayed in the painting?" Although the ultimate objective in the activity is clear (e.g., understanding historical context), the sequence of questioning and probing will depend upon the individual class. Often a decoding activity moves from a few general questions to more specific questions involving a detailed analysis of media messages, and finally to broader understandings of concepts or ideas.

In Chapter 3, we also introduced the key questions for analyzing media messages, which include specific examples of probes (follow-up questions) designed to deepen students' analysis, understanding, and reflection on their own meaning making (see Figure 3.2, p. 44). The probes often ask the students to back up their conclusions or opinions with evidence—and it may be important to clarify that you are looking for evidence *from the document* (rather than from prior knowledge or other experience). Other probes are designed to provoke self-reflection ("Why might that matter to me?" "Why do I think that?") or to encourage further exploration ("What else do I need to know?" "How could we find that out?").

In carrying out a CMD activity, you might decide to probe some responses and not others. For example, you might ask students to give one adjective to describe one of the characters in a media message (e.g., de Soto), offering each student the opportunity to respond before returning to one or two of those responses that are the most intriguing ("What makes you say he's thoughtful?") or that will get you more quickly to your goals ("Why do you think he's revered?"). We've noticed, however, that teachers often fail to probe responses that reflect the "right" or "desired" answer, sometimes just saying "Good!" or "Exactly right!" It's important to guard against doing this, since it's likely to reinforce a sense that you are using the decoding process to guide students toward one correct answer, and as soon as you've gotten it, you can stop the decoding. Nothing is further from the truth. And although you certainly might respond with an affirmative nod or comment, it's important to probe those responses as well. Consider following up on important responses by students ("The painting perpetuates ethnocentrism") with a probe for more clarification ("Can you explain what you mean by that?"). In this way, the teacher can facilitate student-to-student learning of complex ideas through the language of their peers.

The CMD process can and should offer many opportunities for students to respond to the questions. With younger students, this approach can be facilitated by asking them to raise their hands if they agree ("How many people think the target audience for that Hot Wheels commercial was only boys?"), followed by a probe question designed to elicit individual responses ("What makes you say it was only boys?"). You can also flip the process by following up on an individual response or interpretation by saying "Raise your hand if you agree" or "Does anyone disagree?"

One of the most powerful outcomes of this type of question-based media decoding comes when a student gives a response that reflects something you hadn't even noticed yourself. The collective nature of this whole-class decoding fosters learning from each other—including the teacher learning from the students. The follow-up probes themselves can also elicit surprising responses. Remember the example of Cyndy's graduate student from Vietnam described in Chapter 2? When the student was asked which person in the painting she thought was de Soto, she pointed to one of the men behind de Soto instead of the expected response of the man in the middle on the white horse. Cyndy was startled because no one had ever given that (wrong) answer before. But if she had just corrected the student and moved on, she never would have unpacked the cultural perspectives behind the student's selection of the other man, which came through clearly following up with the probing question: "What makes you say *he* is de Soto?" Those teachable moments are quite powerful— especially when we (the teachers) are the ones learning the lesson. As you become more comfortable with the CMD process, you may find yourself automatically building in these types of questions and probes for lessons and activities you've been doing for years.

Easy Tweaks to Integrate CMD into Existing Lessons

There are many simple tweaks you can make to your teaching and lesson design that can incorporate CMD activities while taking little time from your instruction—or your evenings. To begin with, consider adding one or two media literacy questions every day to your students' classroom experiences. Doing so could be as simple as posing one of the key questions for analyzing media messages when you introduce a new piece of media (text, video, image, etc.). After you have been doing this for a while, you can switch to asking your students, "What questions would you want to ask about this (image, text, clip, etc.)"? That, after all, is the ultimate goal: for students to begin asking these questions reflexively in their daily experiences with media, both inside and outside the classroom.

The CMD approach can also be easily integrated into many of the methodologies that teachers use as standard practices. Take the K-W-L approach, for example, that is often used when introducing a new topic or unit: "What do we already **K**now about this?" "What do we **W**ant to know about this?" and (at the end of the unit) "What did we **L**earn about this?" This tool dovetails beautifully with the questions we might ask about the role of media in prior and current learning:

- "What do we already **K**now about this—and where did we learn that? Did we get that idea or information from media sources? Is it true?"
- "What do we **W**ant to know about this—and what types of sources should we use? When would it make sense to get information from a video or a website rather than a book? When might it be best to use a nonmediated source, such as talking to an expert in the field or someone who lived through an event like this?"
- "What did we **L**earn about this—and what sources were the most useful (or the least useful), and why?"

This expanded K-W-L approach was used effectively by one of our local 5th grade teachers, Betty House, who decided to overlay her standard Thanksgiving lesson with CMD analyses. Instead of simply showing a documentary film from her school library to teach the students about the first Thanksgiving, she engaged them in each step of the expanded K-W-L process, coupled with a CMD decoding of the documentary film and four other sources: a children's book, a Native American website, excerpts from pilgrim Edward Winslow's journal, and the 1994 Disney film *Squanto, A Warrior's Tale*. In their final reflection about which sources had been the most and least useful, they decided that all of the media sources were in agreement about the basic events—except for the Disney movie, which focused on violence and conflict between the pilgrims and the Native Americans, including Squanto's "daring escape" from the British. As a class, they concluded that although the Disney film was the most fun to watch, it was also the least accurate source of information about the actual events.

This example illustrates a central tenet of both inquiry based learning and the CMD approach: students learn best when they can explore and gather information, drawing their own conclusions from their investigations. Those elements of self-discovery and surprise provided the foundation for another set of lessons developed by Project Look Sharp in collaboration with a local 3rd grade teacher to introduce a new unit on Africa (Sperry, LaZarre, & Mayer, 2008). The teacher's goals included helping students to learn about the vast diversity of the continent of Africa and to confront their own stereotypes about African cultures and peoples. The resulting lessons (which can be found on the Project Look Sharp website) started by showing the 3rd graders a set of 12 pictures similar to those in Figure 4.3. For each photograph, students were asked to respond on a worksheet to the questions "Do you think this is a picture from Africa? In a few words, why or why not?" The students' responses reflected typical stereotypes about Africa (e.g., pictures featuring elephants or a girl carrying a basket on her head were from Africa, whereas pictures of a modern city or someone using a cell phone were not). Even more illuminating were the words the students used in their decoding of the pictures as definitely *not* from Africa (e.g., "Coca-Cola," "clothes," "city") and definitely *yes* from Africa (e.g., "poor," "dirt," "hut"). Those types of responses are particularly informative for teachers in understanding what assumptions and misconceptions students may be bringing to the study of a different country or culture.

FIGURE 4.3 **Images from Africa**

Are these pictures from Africa? Why or why not?

Name _____ Date _____

1. Yes ☐   No ☐
_____
_____

2. Yes ☐   No ☐
_____
_____

3. Yes ☐   No ☐
_____
_____

4. Yes ☐   No ☐
_____
_____

5. Yes ☐   No ☐
_____
_____

6. Yes ☐   No ☐
_____
_____

Source: All photos courtesy of Pexels.com.

When the students finished their decoding, the teacher told them that all of the pictures were from Africa—and they almost fell off their chairs in astonishment. That experience led to deep conversations about why they didn't have an accurate understanding of the vast diversity of the continent, where their stereotypes had come from (often from the media), and how they could find more current and accurate images and information about African countries. You could use a similar approach when introducing the study of any region, country, or culture, as well as new topics related to science (e.g., "Is this a picture of a volcano?"), health (e.g., "Is this food part of a vegan diet?"), and other curriculum areas.

There are other simple tweaks that will turn your existing lessons into media decoding activities. If you have students prepare book reports, conduct research projects, or explore current events in the news, consider ways that they can also reflect on the constructed nature of the mediated information they notice as an added component of the assignment. Have them reflect on the ways in which the book cover or news headline may be constructed to target a particular audience. When researching issues or news, have students compare the coverage of different media outlets and identify how the language, tone, and content may indicate different biases. If you are showing a documentary film, have students look for content that might reflect particular biases or economic goals of the film's producers (e.g., in health videos about hygiene or puberty, what products are shown, and how are they described?). For research in science, have students reflect on the currency and accuracy of the information and the credibility of their sources. And in all of these activities, encourage students to develop their own questions about the credibility and messages found in the sources they are using.

Alternatives to Whole-Class Decoding

The approach to media decoding we have presented so far has assumed a teacher-led decoding of media with an entire class. Below are some additional approaches that you can use instead of—or to supplement—a whole-class media decoding. They can also be adapted to online learning and in some cases may be more effective when done digitally.

- **Individual decoding for homework.** You can give a media analysis assignment to students as a stand-alone assignment or to prepare them for in-class work.

- **Involving family in media analysis at home.** Students can work at home to find media examples that lend themselves to CMD analyses, coming up with questions to ask about the media messages they've found. Sources could include books and magazines, food and other product packaging, board games, prints and pictures on the walls, TV shows, movies, video games, and the news. You might have them do this together with other family members—an approach that is particularly suited to elementary students.

- **CMD bulletin boards.** Post media examples that you (or better yet, your students) have found, encouraging students to write questions for analysis (and responses) on different-colored sticky notes.

- **Pair/triad work.** When decoding a series of documents, have pairs of students prepare to respond to questions. Doing so can diversify the voices and perspectives typically heard during the decoding.

- **Students leading the decoding.** As students develop more comfort with the decoding process, you can have them generate the questions for analysis or facilitate the decoding themselves. You will need to build in time for them to review documents and background information and develop questions.

- **Students choosing the media documents.** Use students as a research source for media documents that you or they can then decode with the class.

- **Supporting students' unique needs.** Consider using support staff (special ed staff, TESOL, student TAs) to prepare some students for in-class decoding. With added time and support, typically quiet students may even be able to take the lead in a decoding.

CMD and Online Instruction

When we began writing this book in 2020, educators throughout the United States (from kindergarten through college) faced the incredible challenge of quickly transitioning all of their instruction to remote learning, with little to no warning or training. Cyndy faced this situation with her classes at Ithaca College, including for a course that specifically focused on media literacy with a heavy emphasis on constructivist media decoding. Although the challenge was daunting at first, she gradually came to appreciate the ways in which media decoding lent itself to student engagement and to drawing all students (even the introverted ones who never would have raised their hands in an in-person class) into the discussion by posting comments in the chat section. Based on those experiences, along with conversations with K–12 teachers and librarians over the following months, we were able to develop recommendations for actively engaging students in media decoding using both synchronous and asynchronous methods.

Many of the guidelines for doing CMD as part of remote instruction build on the same approaches and tips that we have already explored in this and earlier chapters. For example, it's still important to frame the activity so that students understand the context (including the source of the message, if appropriate), providing relevant background information (if necessary), or reminding them of concepts in previous readings they've done. Ask questions that can engage all students and eventually lead the conversation to your subject-area and media literacy goals. Probe for evidence to back up their comments and interpretations ("Where do you see that?" "What makes you say that?"), which is key to building critical-thinking and reflection skills.

Synchronous Decoding with Students

This type of decoding would likely occur using a videoconferencing tool or a platform online tool such as Zoom or Google Meet that allows for students and educators to interact in real time, discussing topics through a typed chat or verbal conversation and responding to polls or to yes/no questions with raised hands. As with any CMD activity, you would show a short video clip, image, or piece of text, or play an audio clip or music excerpt, and then ask the students questions about what they've seen, read, or heard. Some questions are likely to be specific to the content and your curriculum goals, whereas others will reflect the media literacy objectives raised in earlier chapters (e.g., exploring the source and purpose, techniques used in making the message, credibility, and impact on the audience). When doing these kinds of decodings online, there are some specific guidelines to make them effective:

- **Make sure the media example(s) can be seen or heard clearly** by the students through the platform you are using. It's important to test it out the first time you do this, and you may locate specific settings to enable your device's sound or to optimize videos for the platform you're using. If using Google Meet, for example, you'll want to present a tab, not the whole screen, when showing a video. These are things to troubleshoot before a lesson.
- **If possible, find someone to be your assistant during the decoding.** This person can monitor the chat (and summarize it for you) and keep an eye on the raised hands (calling on students by name, who can then unmute themselves and answer the question). This individual could be a teaching assistant, another teacher or aide, a parent, or even a student in the class. Students who prefer not to share publicly might also be able to send a private message to the assistant, who could share it with the class without naming the student.
- **As you introduce the CMD activity, be clear about what students are being asked to look or listen for, and how they should respond to the questions** (e.g., through the chat or with raised hands). Presenting written instructions can be helpful, as students with poor internet connections may miss verbal instructions.
- **For students in upper-elementary grades and above, make extensive use of the chat function for responses to media**

decoding questions. For some questions, you could ask all students to type responses in the chat box and then follow up with one or two to expand on their responses verbally.

- **If possible, record the media decoding** (and save the written chat responses) so that you can review the contributions for purposes of assessment.

Asynchronous (Preset, Offline) Decoding with Students

Although asynchronous decoding doesn't allow you to engage in real-time back-and-forth probing of student responses, it does have the huge advantage of allowing students to participate in the decoding at any time and to take more time to come up with their responses. Again, you could provide a short video clip, image, or piece of text, or even play an audio clip or music excerpt (e.g., posted on Jamboard, Padlet, or Moodle), then ask questions about that media example that relate to your content and your curriculum goals, as well as media literacy goals. Here are some additional guidelines to follow when creating (and assessing) an asynchronous decoding:

- **Use a platform that will allow you to upload or otherwise share your media example in such a way that your students can easily and clearly see, hear, or read it.** Consider the devices that your students will be using to access the media documents, and be sure that the format you're using will be accessible to them. If it is a still image or a piece of text, it helps if the students can zoom in or increase the size to see details clearly.
- **Provide a written, audio, or video introduction that frames the activity.** Be sure that the students know what they're being asked to look or listen for, how they are expected to respond, and roughly how long their responses to each question should be.
- **Decide if you want students to see (or hear) each other's responses and if you want them to respond directly to each other's comments.** If you don't have a way to do this through your

regular classroom platform, use tools such as VoiceThread, Flipgrid, Padlet, or Poll Everywhere to help you to achieve this goal.

- **Ask one or two general questions that will foster initial involvement, then move on to more specific questions.** Don't pose all the questions at once, but encourage students to answer them one at a time, leading to more specific details and standards-based questions. Depending on your platform, you may want to pose these questions in separate threads.

- **Encourage students to ask their own questions** ("What else would you like to know about this message that would help you judge its credibility?"), **and deepen their analysis by occasionally embedding follow-up probes** ("Describe where you see or hear that in the message," "Give evidence from the media document to support your conclusion"). Provide them with these questions and probes in a place where they can access them.

- **If you are asking students to respond to each other's comments, be clear about your expectations.** It helps to note that you're expecting their additional comments to enrich the conversation by adding new information, bringing in a concept from class, or asking new questions.

Using CMD to Build Home-School Connections

One of the things we hear frequently from the families of students who have been doing CMD activities in the classroom is how often their children talk about what they've learned. This dialogue may happen when discussing current events, shopping at the grocery store, and especially when watching TV shows or movies with the family. Students may point out techniques used to frame a news story, comment on the music or voice-over in a TV commercial, or take the time to read the fine print on a food or toy package. They might also teach their parents, siblings, and other family members some media construction terms and techniques or share what they learned about credibility and bias in the news. We call this the "trickle-up effect," which can be very empowering—especially for young children.

Some of Cyndy's favorite stories have come from her experiences teaching about media literacy and nutrition with children in kindergarten and 1st grade. Using some of Project Look Sharp's lessons as a foundation, the students learn to ask questions about how much sugar is in different cereals and to understand that although fruit is generally a healthful thing to eat, some foods and beverages (such as Apple Jacks, Fruit by the Foot, Kool-Aid, or Cherry 7UP) might pretend to have a lot of fruit in them, but they really don't. The children decode TV commercials for products such as Trix and Fruit Gushers, explore the side panels of cereal boxes to find out the number of grams of sugar in each serving, and learn to recognize the difference between 100 percent juice versus only 5 percent or 10 percent juice. Parents have shared conversations that their children have spontaneously raised at the grocery store ("We should see how much sugar is in that before we buy it." "They're only pretending there's fruit in that; we have to see what's in the ingredients!"). One parent emailed Cyndy to say that her 5-year-old daughter had come home from school saying that she didn't want to eat Fruity Pebbles anymore because the cereal didn't really have any fruit in it and it had a lot of sugar, so she wanted to eat Cheerios instead. The mother happily complied. One morning a few weeks later, the daughter asked for Fruity Pebbles. When the mother responded, "I thought you said that had a lot of sugar in it," her daughter replied, "I shouldn't have told you about that!"—but then asked for the Cheerios.

You can reinforce these CMD home-school connections by regularly sharing information about media the students have been decoding at school and suggesting ways that families can practice media decoding at home. You might even consider sending home the Key Questions handout (Figure 3.2, p. 44) for the whole family to use as they interact with different media and invite them to share stories about what they've noticed about media messages they have encountered and discussed.

You Don't Have to Reinvent the Wheel

As you work to develop new CMD activities for your students, we encourage you to review the format of Project Look Sharp's lessons. The simple but effective template includes clear objectives for the activity, one or more engaging media documents for analysis, key questions to ask throughout the activity, and (sometimes) relevant background information that should be presented to students before, during, or after the decoding. You can also find additional guidance through Project Look Sharp's DIY (Do-It-Yourself) Guide for developing media literacy lessons (https://projectlooksharp.org/diy). Like everything else on our website, that guide is free and reflects many years of working with teachers and librarians at all grade levels to develop effective CMD activities for their unique contexts and students.

One final note. In developing these initial CMD activities—especially if you will be delivering them online or in another challenging context—give yourself (and your students) some time to get the hang of it and to find the approaches that work best for you and for them. The conversations and responses will grow increasingly rich as time progresses, and you may find that you are developing your own habits of inquiry that show up with increasing frequency during the school day.

CHALLENGING CONVERSATIONS
AND MEANING MAKING

At this point in the book, we hope that you are coming to recognize the complexities in the relatively simple process we call constructivist media decoding. On one level we are merely codifying a method for leading the analysis of media messages in the classroom. The complexity comes in the many concerns that need to be addressed in the interest of good teaching.

In this chapter, we will deal with how our biases as teachers affect our media decoding work, the risks and challenges of using potentially harmful documents when addressing charged topics, and how to listen to student meaning making. Although we give guidelines for this work, teaching has no scripts or absolutes, as we are continually mindful of the complex and beautiful diversity of our students' experiences. Add to this the intimidating power of media to both teach and do harm, and we have plenty to consider—even for a five-minute media decoding activity. Ultimately, these cautions and concerns must be held up to your experience as an educator and, most importantly, the experience of your students.

Although we should have been teaching students how to rigorously assess truth claims in the media long before the internet, the tribalization of politics and media require us to explicitly teach about bias. Schools provide the singular domestic space to ensure that future citizens are practiced in the habits of open-mindedness, skepticism, and metacognition. This goal requires that, from the earliest ages, our students are asking well-reasoned questions about authorship, credibility, and bias. These questions should not be pejorative or accusatory but, rather, a normal approach to thinking about mediated messages and about our own thinking.

Dealing with Our Own Biases

In 1979, as a first-year teacher, Chris enthusiastically launched his media literacy unit with the goal of teaching middle schoolers about the misogyny and racism in the popular songs, films, and magazines that they consumed and loved. Almost immediately, a handful of White boys in the class saw their primary task as challenging what they perceived to be Chris's biases against their music and other media. He hadn't yet adopted a constructivist approach to decoding, so his students often responded by saying, "You are reading into this. You just want us to hate our music." They knew that Chris was providing *his own* interpretations rather than guiding the students in *their own* independent thinking. From that experience, Chris learned that the role of the teacher was to choose the documents, ask the questions, and facilitate the decoding, but not to provide the analysis.

Students, particularly adolescents, need to trust that our primary aim is to teach them *how* to think independently, rigorously, and reflectively, but not to teach them *what* to think. Hearing student comments that suggest that we are biased is a great opportunity not only for feedback but also for students to provide evidence to back up their claims: "What makes you say that?" "Where is your evidence?" When students accurately identify how our teaching reflects our biases, their doing so is not necessarily a negative. Their comments may point to the places where we should celebrate our values, such as our biases for critical thinking, fact-based analysis, open-mindedness, or social justice. Bias is not an accusation to be defended against but a reality to be understood.

Media literacy does not ask *if there is a bias* in a media document, but *what the biases are.* All media messages come from a point of view, highlight certain information and leave out other data, include some voices and exclude others, and stress certain values that may benefit some or harm others. Our role as media literacy educators is to teach students to thoughtfully decode these myriad messages, to ask good questions, to make astute evaluations, and to critically reflect on their own interpretations. Students should know that we will challenge them when their thinking is simplistic, unreasoned, factually inaccurate, or otherwise shoddy, but not when their conclusions are just different from ours.

If bias is an inclination or prejudice *against* one thing or certain people and *for* others, we all carry many biases. Some biases, such as racial prejudice, we work as a society to eliminate. But others, such as a bias toward equity or honesty, many readers of this book celebrate and work to deepen.

We acknowledge that this notion runs counter to the use of the word *bias* as exclusively negative, often meaning a prejudiced bigotry against a group. We believe that it is important to recognize that we all have many biases and prejudices that influence our behavior, and that all communication reflects biases. Reserving the term *bias* for only some of our judgments makes others invisible. Therefore, throughout this book we use the word *bias* not as a pejorative but as a descriptor of the views, values, beliefs, attitudes, and interests of media creators.

Bias also applies to our choices as educators. We express our biases, consciously or not, when we design lessons, teach classes, and evaluate students. It is not possible—or even desirable—for us to be free of bias, but it is necessary for us to become perpetually more aware of our biases and how they affect our students. And we need to be explicit about those biases in our teaching.

A key part of the trust we must develop in a classroom depends on students' belief that one of our primary goals is for them to learn to think for themselves. That trust will be built over time through numerous tests of our sincerity. Students, particularly adolescents, will be looking to see where we insert our own biases. This observation can include our choice of media documents to decode. If we consistently facilitate the critical analysis of media examples that reflect one point of view but never critique examples that reflect a contrary perspective, that omission will erode trust, especially for students who hold the opposing perspective. Leading a deep critical analysis of Republican political ads but never Democratic ones would be giving a clear message about what students should feel free to criticize and what not to criticize. Similarly, consistently leading decodings of messages by environmental activists but not messages by oil companies would clearly communicate biases. Assuming that we want our students to think independently, we should have them decode media messages that reflect an appropriate diversity of perspectives and values.

We also express our biases in *how* we lead a decoding. Here are two examples of framing a media decoding of a political advertisement:

Framing #1: "This two-minute video clip was used to introduce candidate George W. Bush at the 2000 Republican convention. I want you to look for the messages about candidate Bush and the techniques used by the filmmakers to craft Bush's image."

Framing #2: "Here is how the Republicans tried to present Bush at their convention. Look for the tricks they used to spin his image as an 'everyman' and a 'good ole boy.'"

The words we choose in framing a document indicate to students how we want them to interpret the document. Our body language and verbal cues also communicate our biases. When we guffaw or *tsk* at a particular text (we call this a "danger cluck"), we are telling our students what is safe to say in the classroom and what is not. These messages undermine students' trust that we welcome divergent views. It is likely that our biases in tone, language, and affect will be most evident to students who do not share our perspectives and potentially invisible to students who do.

When this issue emerged during an extensive professional development session with educators in 2000, we decided to lead a highly biased decoding of the Bush biographical video just mentioned to illustrate this point. In leading the decoding, Chris went overboard with danger clucks, eye rolling, and highly biased language ("You won't believe how deceptive this film is!" "Look for ways Bush's handlers manipulated his image."). As Chris led the decoding and the participants got more and more into it, we were sure they were all in on the joke. When the decoding ended, however, one of the participants said, "That was the best decoding yet!" He was not joking and did not realize that we were presenting a negative model for a CMD. It is natural for people who have strong political positions to enthusiastically support an analysis that reflects their passions, even if we have been talking explicitly about checking one's biases. You will need to assess for yourself when you will need to be particularly conscious of not imposing your thinking on students.

We can also limit students' ability to think creatively and independently by limiting the scope of our questioning. Many times we have seen teachers lead a decoding so targeted to a particular answer from students that the teacher responds to student analysis by saying, "No, that is not it." If our probing is so specific that students must hunt for what we want them to say, we are not asking the right questions. If our choice of documents for analysis is so limited that it sets up binary choices that do not reflect the complexity of an issue, then we are not providing students with the opportunity to think deeply. If our leading of the decoding makes it clear what the right answers are, we are not teaching independent thinking.

Students should know that we will hold them accountable for complex and open-minded thinking and that we will challenge their thinking when it is weak. In general, their critical thinking will be sharp when they are decoding messages that challenge their biases but dull when they are analyzing messages that confirm their biases. Our task as educators is to challenge students when their critical thinking is dull, especially when it reflects the biases within our community—often the biases we hold dear.

When Project Look Sharp was developing new lessons on sustainability (Sperry, 2014), we brought together a group of scientists and environmental activists for a charette (an advising session) on lesson creation. We had them analyze the children's book *The Truax* (Birkett, 1994), published by the National Wood Flooring Manufacturers' Association, which is a take-off on Dr. Seuss's environmental classic, *The Lorax* (Seuss, 1971). In *The Truax*, the environmentalist is portrayed as a fanatic, while the logger brings data, science, and facts to back up his arguments. When we asked the scientists to decode *The Truax*, they quickly identified the distortions and exaggerations implied in the book (e.g., that logging prevents forest fires and protects endangered species). But when we had the scientists and activists decode *The Lorax*, which for many of them was an original inspiration for their career choice and identity, they all thought that the information was quite accurate! In fact, *The Lorax* also contains several factual distortions, implying, for example, that clear cutting kills *all* life in a forest. These highly educated women and men, nearly all of whom had advanced degrees in science, were limited in their critical-thinking capacities when analyzing a cherished media document that confirmed their own collective biases.

Teaching Challenging Topics

Constructivist media decoding is particularly effective when working with challenging, controversial, or otherwise "hot" topics. The process of inquiry-based facilitation gives teachers the tools to lead a rigorous analytical discussion about a charged topic with some academic distance. For instance, if we want students to grapple with their own biases related to race and racism and we have a racially mixed class with divergent opinions, asking students to give document-based responses to specific questions can help ensure greater safety in the classroom by providing boundaries to their comments. Showing a racially charged media document—say, a political advertisement about immigration—and asking, "What is your reaction?" or "What does this bring up for you?" invites potentially hurtful responses. Asking, "What are the messages here about immigrants, and what is your evidence?" can help to keep the comments more academic and text-based. This approach enables us to move toward the most challenging and important conversations over time, assessing safety along the way, particularly for the most vulnerable and marginalized students.

The choice of media documents provides another opportunity to move cautiously into challenging material with students. Sticking with the previous example, it might be wise to start the discussion of immigration by choosing a media document that has some historical distance for students. Contemporary media documents often have the added power of personal context. Analyzing a historical immigration ad is likely to be less charged emotionally for students than a current advertisement. In either case, keeping the analysis document-based provides greater teacher control over the discussion. Although we aim to have students reflect on their own biases—including their origins, their limitations, and the effect they can have on others—setting up this type of learning will require time, trust, and openness.

Another important concern when planning and leading a media decoding is the unintended and unpredictable consequences of decoding potentially harmful media documents. Although we may agree that we want our classrooms to be open to divergent perspectives, our tolerance is challenged when students raise hurtful perspectives related to issues of identity. In these situations, we may need to break our impartiality and intervene in order to protect our students. Some of the most difficult moments as media literacy educators come when we must—on the spot— weigh how to limit the potential negative impact of students' comments.

Our commitment to being impartial when leading a decoding stops when a student says something that is hurtful to other students. This possibility becomes more likely and riskier when decoding documents that may elicit racist, sexist, classist, homophobic, or ableist responses. When analyzing media documents that raise issues of religious, gender, geographic, political, or other identities, we must be prepared to intervene to protect the safety of students, particularly those most marginalized and vulnerable. Although our tendency in leading a media decoding is to support divergent perspectives and to encourage students to challenge each other's views, there are times when the teacher, not the students, has the responsibility to challenge a particular comment. When a student says something that is clearly hurtful and prejudiced, it is the adult's responsibility to step in and address what was said.

There is no script for this moment, and we will likely rerun it many times in our mind, searching for the right response. All media literacy teachers find themselves in this spot frequently if they are drawn to dealing with challenging issues. Although there are no absolutes, here are some general guidelines:

- **Establish ground rules for discussions** early in the year and return to them as needed. Such rules should include addressing laughter, mocking, side comments, or crosstalk. Ideally, involve students in this process.
- **When planning to decode challenging material, think through your potential responses** to hurtful or inappropriate comments.
- **Respond when someone is being hurtful,** making it clear that you will take responsibility by intervening. Do not remain silent or leave it up to students to respond.
- **Try to avoid shaming a student, but clearly address the harm.** By depersonalizing the comment ("Sometimes we can say things that are hurtful without even knowing it"), we can respond without overtly calling out the individual student ("That was a terrible thing to say").
- **Follow up the discussion with individual students,** listening to their experience as you plan a path forward, but do not put any responsibility on anyone targeted by the comment.
- **Check in with advisors,** particularly those who can shed light on the experience of students who are most marginalized in your class.
- **Integrate responses to the situation into your future teaching.** How can you construct your classroom and curriculum to address the roots of the comments before they are voiced?

For Chris, one of the most painful experiences in his 40 years of teaching occurred early in his career. It began with the response from a few students to disturbing images from the Holocaust. Some Jewish students in the class felt their peers were mocking the victims. That night, Chris was contacted by a parent who asked for a meeting. This parent was the child of Holocaust survivors. Chris began the meeting by apologizing for how uncomfortable the situation was. The father immediately shot back, "Don't you dare apologize for the discomfort! I sat through classes my whole childhood where teachers hurried to get past the Holocaust as quickly as possible to avoid the discomfort. Studying the Holocaust should never be comfortable!" It was in that conversation that Chris began to understand the distinction between comfort and safety. Although it is important to strive to create a classroom space and relationships that are safe for all students, when dealing with these deep, emotional, and painful issues, we should not be striving for comfort.

As much as we plan to address situations that may emerge as we delve into challenging issues with our students, we must prepare ourselves to make mistakes and to learn from them. Sometimes we cannot avoid painful moments. The pain often reflects the historical trauma behind the images, sounds, and words. Often there is no "right" way to respond. But entering into the conflict with humility, checking our defensiveness, and listening compassionately to the experiences of others is a good place to start.

It would be easier to steer clear of these situations by avoiding using media that can provoke such emotion. And, at times, avoidance is the prudent call. But students are often seeing, hearing, and reading these media messages without any adult facilitation. Our choices about what to bring into our classrooms require both courage and caution.

The Limits to Questioning

In any school, as in any culture, analysis has limits—things that we *do not* put up for question. The student-centered, progressive school where Chris taught for many years prides itself on critical thinking but would never consider inviting someone to present a neo-Nazi perspective to students. Certain perspectives should not be entertained, and certain questions fall outside the boundary of appropriateness. We would never ask our students to debate the pros and cons of slavery, the Holocaust, or the Trail of Tears. Human consensus that genocide is wrong places those debates outside acceptable questioning, lest we communicate that there is an actual debate to be had.

But what about colonialism? In 2004, most 10th graders in New York State were asked to write a document-based essay on the positive and negative effects of colonialism for the Regents Exam in Global History (NYSED, 2004). Was that appropriate? Would it be appropriate for students to decode media documents that present conflicting perspectives on the science of evolution, climate change, or vaccines? Should elementary-age students debate the appropriateness or even morality of eating "junk" foods that are a staple in many families?

Different issues will fall inside and outside the boundaries of acceptable questioning in different schools, communities, and nations. When we led decodings in Iran in 2015, we were encouraged to have teachers engage their students in passionate analysis of "gender issues," but we were told in no uncertain terms that any analysis related to "sexuality" was taboo. In Turkey, we were told to stay away from Turkish politics in all forms and to avoid speaking the names *Kurdish* (referring to the ethnic group) or *Erdoğan* (referring to the president of Turkey). But we were encouraged to work with teachers to decode media messages about issues that had national consensus, such as "domestic violence."

These boundaries are not limited to other countries. One U.S. teacher told us that she could not possibly use the lessons in our kit titled *Media Construction of War* in her school because it was on a military base, and questioning war was not acceptable. Some of Project Look Sharp's lessons on global warming have been criticized because they use documents that question the human causes of climate change. Every teacher will need to decide the risks and benefits of decoding a particular document in the school's specific context.

The documents we choose (and exclude) for analysis, the questions we ask (and don't ask), and the places we probe (and choose not to probe) reflect our values, proprieties, and boundaries. It is not a question of whether to teach critical thinking, but where we will ask students to question and where we will refrain from enabling questioning. Would it be appropriate to ask our students to debate the pros and cons of racism? We suggest that this is an inappropriate question at any age and in any contemporary context because it proposes that racism is an acceptable choice. Would it be appropriate to have high school students analyze different perspectives on the Black Lives Matter movement or on affirmative action policies? Likely yes, as these issues involve current and evolving thinking within our culture that needs adult facilitation for civil dialogue to help us perceive complexity and understanding from multiple points of view. But which perspectives get legitimized for discussion in our classroom is a critical issue. Would we bring a White supremacist perspective on civil rights into the classroom? Likely not. Are there situations when analyzing documents about issues of race would be inappropriate? Most definitely. If students are too young to understand the complexities, or the environment is too polarized for healthy conversation, or the context is not safe to do the analysis, then we should not decode any of these documents—at least for now.

Constructivist media decoding can and should be used to teach uncontroversial subjects as well. Few schools would deny the importance of having students critically analyze the credibility of different sources of information, although they might disagree on the conclusions. Nearly all schools support having students learn to discern accurate versus deceptive messages about healthy eating or concepts in physics or graphical representations of data. We have consensus that critical thinking about facts, the ability to identify bias, and the ability to ask good, well-reasoned questions are an essential part of a good education. What is debated is what we apply that critical questioning to and what we do not question. One arena where we tend to have agreement, at least in the United States, is the need to address negative stereotypes perpetuated by media messages.

Dealing with Stereotypes

Mass media provide a fertile platform for spreading overly generalized and often malicious messages about certain people. Throughout history, media have been used in perpetuating acts of unspeakable injustice, from the use of minstrel shows and caricatures to spread White supremacy in the United States to the use of radio to galvanize anti-Tutsi genocide in Rwanda in 1993. We can sometimes use stereotypical messages to teach students about that history and the dangers of dehumanizing people, but we must always be aware of the risks and dangers of using hurtful media messages in our classrooms.

In 2004, Project Look Sharp was working with educators in the Ithaca City School District to develop a media literacy component for the new 3rd grade curriculum on Africa. The advisory group included Peyi Soyinka-Airewele, a parent who taught politics at Ithaca College and who is from Nigeria. When Chris shared some media literacy curriculum material used at the high school level to teach about stereotypes, Peyi had a visceral response: "Above all else, you must *do no harm* to my children!" The intensity of her plea was a wakeup call for us and our work. She went on to explain that our *intention* of teaching students to critically analyze stereotypes made no difference if we ultimately reinforced those stereo- types. Peyi said that presenting 3rd graders with *any* racist imagery, even in a critical context, would likely reinforce those messages and damage her children's views of Africa and of themselves. Her heartfelt challenge to our best intentions was a gift to Project Look Sharp.

Ultimately, Peyi's feedback helped us to develop the *Understanding Africa* kit and lessons described in Chapter 4. It also caused us to rethink our high school curriculum. We continue to use racist images with sec- ondary students to analyze historical messages about race and power, the impact of those messages, and the role of media in perpetuating sys- tems of slavery, colonialism, and White supremacy. Peyi felt that a well- constructed high school curriculum could repurpose racist images for critical analysis, but that derogatory and stereotypical representations needed to be contrasted with images that presented a more complex, human, and full representation of Africans. Following Peyi's advice, we researched and added a series of new media documents to our high school lessons that contradicted racist stereotypes while engaging students in critical thinking about representation, authorship, perspective, and impact as well as understanding historical context. An example of one of those documents is shown in Figure 5.1.

FIGURE 5.1 Portrait of Joseph Cinqué

Joseph Cinqué was the leader of a slave revolt on the ship *La Amistad* in 1839. He was captured by U.S. forces and tried for mutiny and murder. In one of the most famous trials in U.S. history, the Supreme Court ruled that Cinqué and other Africans were justified in their actions because they were legally free men when they revolted on the high seas. In 1840, Cinqué and 35 others were returned to Sierra Leone. Abolitionist and artist Nathaniel Jocelyn painted the original version of this portrait in 1839, 15 years before the end of slavery in the United States.

Source: By John Sartain (copy after Nathaniel Jocelyn), c. 1840. National Portrait Gallery, Smithsonian Institution. Public domain.

Pause to Reflect

What questions would you ask students about the painting in Figure 5.1 if your goals were for them to understand historical perspective and point of view? What background information would you present? And in what sequence would you present the questions and information?

Developing even very short decoding activities can model the creativity, thoughtfulness, and insight that go into quality teaching. Such teaching includes deciding the objectives for the activity; for instance, *students will apply their knowledge of the history of slavery and abolition, they will understand historical perspective and point of view, and they will practice using evidence to back up their analysis.* Thoughtful decoding considers the precise questions we will ask and in what sequence, and it considers when and where to include information critical to the learning.

Background information does not need to be presented at the beginning of a decoding activity but can be given along the way or can emerge from students' analysis of the document. For instance, by asking students, "Do you think that this is a positive or a negative representation of Cinqué?" and probing for evidence, students are likely to identify the many ways in which this painting presents the subject with dignity and power. Whereas older students may be able to identify the use of classical imagery (toga and staff), younger students may cue into body language, muscle tone, and the background imagery to discuss Cinqué's power. Once students have explored the dignified nature of this representation, the teacher might then tell the story of Cinqué, the *Amistad*, and the trial. Then the teacher could ask, "Why might Nathaniel Jocelyn have painted this portrait in 1839?" If a student were to venture that Jocelyn was an abolitionist (he was), the teacher could ask the student to explain their thinking to the class. In this way, the students in the class can collectively teach one another complex understandings about authorship, point of view, representation, politics, and U.S. history in a way that minimizes the likelihood for hurtful comments.

It is important to note that Peyi's feedback to Project Look Sharp was pivotal in helping us to rethink our work when dealing with issues of race and stereotypes. Her caution to *do no harm* has become a touchstone as we deal with challenging topics. It is no coincidence that this advice came from a woman who is African and African American, a mom, and a professor of politics. It's important to turn to advisors with diverse life experiences and perspectives when doing difficult work with issues of identity.

And we should check our understandable tendency to become defensive when confronted by criticism. When parents, students, colleagues, and others take the risk of giving us critical feedback on our teaching, we can see it as a threat or a gift. That point was particularly true in the next story.

Protecting the Science

In the fall of 2019, two environmental activists and college professors leveled a critique of a few Project Look Sharp lessons that used climate-denial media documents—in particular, a clip from the documentary *The Great Global Warming Swindle* (see the lesson *What Is Causing Global Warming?* on the Project Look Sharp website: https://projectlooksharp.org/causeglobalwarming). They felt that it was inappropriate and potentially dangerous for Project Look Sharp to include the climate-denial perspective even if the lesson in question is designed to have students debunk disinformation. They feared that these types of lessons might inadvertently perpetuate lies and legitimize intentionally distorted ideas promoted by powerful economic and political interests. They felt that the stakes were too high to allow debate that includes positions based on a stance against science. This critique pushed us to better define our approach when using disinformation or potentially harmful media messages in our lessons.

New communication technologies have accentuated the political and cultural polarization of modern societies, leading to a flood of "alternative facts" that undermine traditional authorities and pave the way for the delegitimization of science. The traditional approach of sticking to the facts and letting the science speak for itself is no longer enough. We must take the time to educate students in how to think well, how to reason, and how to evaluate what is true, what is "true-ish," what is biased, what is misleading, what is distorted, and what are outright lies. For students to apply habits of critical thinking to the world of science, science education must bring the world of mediated messaging into the science classroom.

Students need a science curriculum that teaches them to do the following:

- Genuinely explore, discover, and own for themselves fundamental principles of science (the importance of the scientific process, the role of peer review, being open to new evidence, etc.).
- Habitually ask key questions about all media messages, including questions about sourcing, purpose, and the economics behind media messages.
- Rigorously evaluate the credibility, accuracy, and bias in media messages that reflect the ideas (and propaganda) they encounter daily in the media.
- Thoughtfully reflect on their own biases and how those affect their interpretations—how confirmation bias can limit critical thinking and their ability to see complexity.

To achieve these goals, we developed three guidelines to consider when planning science lessons that use misleading or distorted media:

1. **Plan and lead lessons so that students ultimately recognize any distortion or inaccuracies in the science.** If the goal is to teach students the skills, knowledge, and habits of independently identifying credible science, it is best to facilitate their discovery of misinformation through genuine inquiry. Therefore, in our own work we typically refrain from telling our students what information is false—at least at first—and instead use questions to guide their inquiry and understanding. But educators must be conscious of not inadvertently perpetuating dated or distorted science. Our teaching should help students to better distinguish accurate from inaccurate science through their own analysis.

2. **Create lessons that teach students to recognize bias in multiple forms.** These forms include the biases of different stakeholder groups, including industry, activists, and consumers; the biases of those in power who sometimes obfuscate and raise questions to sow doubt; the biases in the media, including false equivalence, didactic polarization, and stoking fear and uncertainty; and our own confirmation biases that cause us to discredit information and sources

that contradict our views and uncritically accept ideas and authors that align with those views.

3. **Be clear on the complexities.** These include distinguishing between social and scientific controversies. Although the science behind the anthropogenic causes of climate change, or the link between vaccines and autism, or the theory of evolution are arguably resolved in the (never closed) world of science, the social, political, and religious debates rage on. In addition, we need to acknowledge the complexity of science. Even well-informed scientists—and science teachers—are often confounded by data, different facts, varied interpretations, and conflicting views. It is important to be transparent about the limits of our understanding. Then the focus of our teaching can be on helping students to learn to navigate ambiguity, embrace complexity, manage uncertainty, and distinguish between what we can know scientifically and what is currently beyond our understanding.

Media decoding in the science classroom, as in all subject areas, requires that teachers make decisions about what media documents are appropriate for their students, what problems are too simple or too complex, what questions will address the essential knowledge that students are on the cusp of understanding, and how to provoke the epistemological disequilibrium that enables students to grow their thinking. Although trusting teachers to do this work may involve risks, *not* teaching students to inquire about what to believe is a greater risk. We need to train and trust educators to adapt any approaches that are not in the best interests of their students and a good education. To do this, teachers need to listen well to their students' meaning making.

Listening to Student Meaning Making

In the late 1980s, Chris invited a filmmaker to his school to screen her documentary to a group of about 80 middle and high school students.

The film was about eating disorders, and it included segments in which young women described their anorexia and bulimia and how it nearly ruined their lives. The discussion following the film was honest and powerful. The event certainly seemed like it had achieved its goal of promoting mental health. After the discussion, a young woman, who Chris knew had struggled with an eating disorder, came up to him and shared, "I love these films. The girls they interview are so thin and beautiful. This is where I learn all my techniques." Despite the best intentions on the part of the filmmaker and the teacher, this film had unintended consequences for at least one student. Although we can never know ahead of time the impact of the media we show and decode, we must always be listening well to how our students understand and interpret the media we bring into our classrooms.

Above all else, successful media decoding, like successful teaching, requires that we constantly assess how our students learn. We can hear it in their words, observe it on their tests, see it in their writing, and feel it in their body language. We can learn from what is shared and what is missing, from their realizations and their confusion, from their participation and their resistance. And we can enlist our students in the collective process of improving learning by continually asking them for feedback about what worked well in our classrooms and what didn't.

Early in his career, Chris was teaching an English lesson on literary elements (e.g., plot, setting, characterization, point of view) and techniques (e.g., irony, metaphor, symbolism). As he began the lesson, he could see his students' eyes begin to glaze over. Teaching in an alternative school with a democratic philosophy, Chris was used to engaging students in decision making about all aspects of teaching and learning, so he stopped the lesson and asked, "What is going on? You guys all just checked out." One of the more academic students in the class responded, "We have been learning about this since 1st grade. Teachers keep going over the same thing every year. We got it." Chris then turned to one of the students in the class who struggled with all aspects of writing about literature and asked what was going on for him. "We did this every year since elementary school. It didn't work for me then, and it doesn't work for me now." Chris could sense resentment and even anger in the student's response.

Chris came to class the next day with an activity borrowed from media literacy expert Frank Baker (Considine & Baker, 2006). Using the first two-and-a-half minutes of the movie *A Beautiful Mind,* Chris asked half the class to look for how the filmmaker developed the main character played by Russell Crowe. He asked the rest to pay attention to the setting or plot or point of view. He wrote the words *imagery, camera angle, lighting, dialogue, acting,* and *sound* on the board and asked the students to be prepared to explain how the filmmaker used these techniques to develop their element (plot, character, etc.).

After showing the clip, Chris asked the group that was analyzing character development, "What were the messages about the Russell Crowe character?" With probing questions from Chris, the students were able to describe in detail the scene in which the lead character mentally drifts away from the party as he sees the repeated patterns in the lemons, crystal goblet, and gaudy tie. The students identified the filmmaker's use of lighting, subtle sounds, background dialogue, body language, and camera movement to construct a story about the unorthodox but beautiful mind of the lead character. Next, the group looking at *point of view* identified how the camera angles let the viewers know that they are seeing the scene through the eyes of the main character. The group that was analyzing the *setting* described the use of color, dialogue, and historical context (e.g., the cigarette smoking) to set the tone of upper-class, White male elitism at Princeton University in 1947. The remaining students used details from the short clip to successfully predict some of the main elements in the plotline. Finally, Chris helped the students to connect what they just did with the film to the analysis of literature and the upcoming essay assignment.

The goal of the engaging and rigorous analysis of a clip from a feature film was to teach all students about literary elements and techniques. From listening to students, Chris knew that he had to approach the lesson from a different angle than he had in his earlier attempt. He suspected that previous lessons on literary elements had been pedagogically traumatic for at least one student. And he knew that he needed to approach this activity in a way that avoided, if not undermined, the academic polarization that existed in the class between the more engaged and the less engaged students. Chris knew from his own experience that approaching the analysis of literature through another medium could give some students the ability to demonstrate their cognitive strengths without being derailed by a frustrating history of struggles with more traditional text-based approaches. And he suspected the lesson would be fun for all students. Indeed, it proved to be quite successful and became a regular tool in Chris's curriculum for the next decade. It was prompted by listening to the meaning making of his students and asking them for help.

Having Flexible Objectives

We have already stressed the importance of having clear objectives when leading a media decoding. Now we want to add some nuance to that guideline and stress the importance of flexibility. It is critical to know where you want to go in a media decoding activity, but it is equally important to follow the lead of students as to what path they take in their analysis. A good example of this can be seen in the 11-minute video demonstration of media decoding titled *The Great Global Warming Swindle* (see Demonstration Videos on the Project Look Sharp website at https://projectlooksharp.org/videos). It demonstrates Chris leading a question-based analysis of the documentary clip mentioned earlier in this chapter.

The decoding starts off just where Chris intends, with students identifying details in the video that illustrate messages about carbon dioxide and the techniques that the filmmaker used to discredit the anthropogenic nature of climate change. But then one 10th grade student takes the analysis in a different direction, saying:

> What I think is interesting is actually our reactions to it [the clip]. Because we all have a lot of opinions on this topic, so we think that our opinion is the right opinion. So as soon as we see something challenging that, we are immediately going to start to say that it is propaganda or start disregarding

it. And I think we could do that for a video, you know, *An Inconvenient Truth,* that is supporting our opinion, mainly. We could look at that and start calling that propaganda as well. And, I mean, personally I really dislike this video. I think that there is a lot of bias, but the immediate thing that comes to mind is, OK, who made this, what is their purpose in making this, what are my own biases and how is that informing my opinion of this video.

Viewing this clip during a professional development session, one educator commented, "It was too bad that that girl diverted you from the point of the lesson." Chris could not disagree more. Although the student did divert him from his plans, she provided a rich opportunity to redirect the lesson to one of the key objectives of his teaching: to have students internalize habits of critical questioning about their own thinking. Although he had not intended to have this lesson be about confirmation bias, she pushed him and the class to go there. Her comment was far from irrelevant or disconnected; it was just not where he had planned to go at that moment.

When facilitating constructivist media decoding activities, as in leading all discussions, we need to make many decisions about which student comments to pass by or even interrupt, which to probe into, and which to linger on. The 10th grader's insightful comments gave Chris the opportunity to have the class pause and identify some of the key questions for media analysis. When she "diverted" the lesson, Chris was able to see how her comments could help to address the longer-term objectives for student learning, even if they were not planned as part of that activity. Spontaneous and independent thinking by students is at the core of student-centered decoding. At times, we won't be able to follow their lead—and at times we shouldn't; but we should always add their comments into our reservoir of data about student meaning making so that we can better integrate their learning into our curricular scope and sequence and into the authentic learning experience of our students.

At the beginning of this chapter, we shared a story about the disastrous beginning of Chris's unit on race, gender, and class in 1979, when he provoked middle school students into mutiny by attempting to "teach" them to critique their own media diet. By listening to their resistance, Chris was forced to rethink his approach to leading media analysis. He knew that his students were fully capable of rigorous and complex analysis into the potentially harmful messages in the media they were consuming, but the analysis needed to come from them. He dropped the hard-hitting films that provided the antiracist and antisexist analysis of youth media, held off on having the students bring in their own media, and began with having students provide their own analysis of gendered advertisements from the early 1900s. As students critiqued the dated messages about gender and class, they began developing critical language and skills in visual analysis. By the time Chris had his students bring in their own media messages, they could not help but apply that analysis to their own media. Chris's role became facilitator of the discussion rather than provider of the analysis.

Celebrating Independent Thinking

When we hear students saying things to us such as "You are reading into this," it is a good indicator that we may be providing the analysis ourselves —or at least our students see it that way. Conversely, when students begin to raise questions about our choices in the curriculum—the textbook we use, the films we show, and the posters on our walls—it is a good indicator that they are learning to be authentically media literate. During the Middle East unit in Chris's high school humanities class, he gave students a 10-page handout on the history of the Israel–Palestine conflict that he had painstakingly written to bring forward divergent perspectives. Almost immediately, the student who was researching Palestinian perspectives on the conflict in preparation for an upcoming debate shouted, "This handout is so biased." Rather than being offended, Chris quickly responded, "OK. Come to class tomorrow with your evidence." The next day, the student assertively slapped her marked-up handout on the table and exclaimed, "I found 16 ways in which this history is anti-Palestinian." The student sitting next to her who was researching Israeli perspectives for the debate spoke up: "And I have 23 ways that this history is anti-Israeli." This launched a powerful discussion of historical objectivity led by the impressive insights of 10th graders.

Ultimately, our success as teachers will be determined by how well we can learn from our students about how they understand the world, how they manage their own learning, and how they make meaning. Our lesson plans should be littered with notes about what worked and what didn't, and, in particular, how we think we could do it better next time. Teaching is an always evolving and infinitely complex art because our students are always changing. One of our primary aims should be to have our students take as much responsibility and joy as possible for constructing their own learning. Chris's most cherished compliment as a teacher came from a struggling student when reflecting on his learning at the end of the year. After listening to his peers' reflections, the student said, "You guys are so much more articulate than me, I don't think there is anything I could add. But... in most classes *I study equations,* but in this class, *I was the equation.*"

ASSESSMENT AND METACOGNITION

As educators, we understand the key role that assessment plays in driving the content and form of our teaching. When we hold students accountable for demonstrating certain knowledge and skills, we hold ourselves accountable for teaching that knowledge and those skills. Assessment takes many forms, from the questions we ask and the observations we make in class, to our own quizzes and high-stakes state tests.

This chapter explores the role media analysis can play in formative and summative assessment. It begins with reflections on the role of CMD in helping us to assess the meaning making of our students, both individually and collectively. It looks at different models for assessing both subject knowledge and critical-thinking skills and ends with an example of an assessment of students' abilities to ask questions and reflect on their own thinking. We believe that if we regularly and effectively assessed these media literacy skills, we would have a more discerning citizenry.

Formative Assessment

Constructivist media decoding activities can always be used for formative assessment. As we ask content and critical-thinking questions and probe for evidence, we are asking students to apply knowledge to their analysis, provide document-based evidence to back up their interpretations, and demonstrate a range of critical-thinking skills. This exercise gives us important information about how well students have internalized the content of the class, if they can use that knowledge in different contexts, and the extent to which they can apply important cognitive skills to the analysis and evaluation of different media messages. The CMD process facilitates a formative evaluation of both our students' abilities and the effectiveness of our teaching.

One of the most salient requirements for good teaching is to consistently gather data on what works and what does not, looking for patterns of success and adapting our curriculum, methodologies, and interactions accordingly. To be successful, our data-gathering tools need to be diverse and their use continual. When students are unable to connect the knowledge we have taught them to the decoding of a particular document, we learn something about the effectiveness of that teaching. When students can apply the knowledge but do not have the critical-thinking skills to see certain perspectives, we learn about the work we must do. When knowledgeable and skilled thinkers cannot generate their own questions, we are pushed to consider a new objective for our curriculum. Media decoding is not only an effective tool in formative assessment of our own teaching; it also gives us critical insights into the meaning making of our students.

When we elicit student interpretations of a media message, we gather data on how students see the world. We hear their language, their observations, their way of making meaning. This can cue us in to not only the uniqueness of each student but also patterns in the interpretations of our students as a group. It can help us to assess where our students have a good understanding of a particular concept or have generally mastered a skill. Conversely, it can let us know where they are missing knowledge or abilities. And it helps us to see the key areas of disequilibrium in which some students have mastered certain understandings and others have not. This formative assessment can help us to focus on these areas of growth through the process of constructivist teaching.

When a student makes an astute observation during a decoding and you ask the class, "Raise your hand if you agree," you are facilitating a formative assessment. If students are paying attention and prepared for this level of interactivity, their response can tell you a lot. If all hands shoot up quickly, it is likely that you do not need to pause on this concept. If no hands go up, it may be worth taking time to assess whether the class understands the question or the concept. If you decide that this concept is within the reach of your students and worth your time to address, and at least one student has a good grasp of the idea, you can ask that student to elaborate on what they see, what they understand. This shifts the role of the teacher from deliverer of knowledge to facilitator of a collaborative and constructivist process of learning.

Assessing and Facilitating Meaning Making

The CMD process, facilitated by a teacher, enables students to hear concepts explained by their peers from a developmental level closer to their own. When a 12-year-old student who has recently mastered a complex concept explains their understanding in their own words, the explanation may be more likely to move the student's peers to a higher level of understanding, both cognitive and affective, than an explanation by a teacher. That student typically has an experiential grasp of their peers' disequilibrium in a different way than the informed but developmentally distanced teacher. This observation suggests that we can be more effective in teaching students important concepts that they are on the cusp of understanding by facilitating dialogue between them, by asking students who have more complex levels of understanding to share their thinking with their peers.

During a professional development workshop demonstrating the CMD process, an undergraduate teacher education student proclaimed, "This is a lot easier than teaching. All you need to do is ask questions." The student failed to see the deep complexity of the constructivist process, in which the teacher is continually listening, assessing, and deciding where, when, and how to probe for understanding; when to ask a student to elaborate; when to ask for a different perspective; where to add key information; when to probe for evidence from the document; when to just let a comment go; and in rare instances, when to challenge a comment directly. This approach to teaching is certainly not "easier" than traditional stand-and-deliver methodology, but it can be far more engaging, rewarding, and effective for both the students and the teacher.

When we probe for understanding of a rich media document, we unearth student meaning making that can inform us, if we listen, about our students' ways of seeing the world. Although each student has a unique life experience that distinguishes their perspective from that of every other person, we need to pay attention to patterns in student responses that help us to understand the overall role of identity in meaning making. When the majority of females in our class tend to have a different interpretation or response to a particular media document than the bulk of the males, that situation is worth noting. The same is true for identities related to race, ethnicity, sexuality, religion, or any of the other deep affiliations that shape our students' meaning making.

At the school where Chris taught for more than 40 years, geography, race, and class often played a big role in students' views of themselves and the world. Rural White students, particularly males from economically marginalized families, tended to have different views from the more academic and urban students, both White students and students of color. Facilitating respectful dialogue between these sometimes disparate groups was both a challenge and an opportunity.

The ability to bridge gaps of understanding and identity so that our students can learn from each other is a core challenge in this work. The many complexities in facilitating a truly student-centered CMD process reflect the beauty and art of teaching. As discussed in the last chapter, the academic analysis of media messages, with its document-based focus and targeted questions, can enable us to facilitate well-bounded discussions on difficult topics between students with diverse identities. Because it is grounded in students' own analysis of relevant media content and its application to their lived experiences, this process also supports the development of higher-order thinking skills identified by McTighe and Silver (2020) as core to deeper learning.

By continually assessing the responses of all students and listening well to their meaning making, we can prepare the curriculum to lead to deeper understandings for all of them. We can use the CMD process to assess when and where we need to move slowly or quickly, what understandings we need to develop over time, what scaffolding needs to be built in, which individual students need coaching, and where we need to be particularly careful. This process is infinitely complex and rarely comfortable, but it can be both safe and effective for deep and internalized learning. And it makes the process of teaching a profoundly rewarding practice.

Summative Assessment

Although media decoding can always support formative assessment of both the students and the activities, sometimes we want and need to administer summative assessments to determine our students' knowledge and skills. There are many types of summative assessment, but they tend to be more quantitative than formative assessments and typically are used to evaluate the skills and knowledge of individual students. One of the advantages of formal summative assessments is that they focus on the demonstrable skills and knowledge that we—or the state—deem most important. When we have the opportunity to make our own summative assessments, we can become creative in developing new ways to integrate media analysis and critical thinking into traditional assessments of knowledge and skills.

We can make summative assessments more accessible to more students by diversifying the types of texts used in our tests. By using non–print-based documents for both information and analysis in assessments, we can enfranchise a greater number of students to be able to more effectively demonstrate what they know and can do. For instance, when assessing a student's understanding of literary elements and techniques, we can use a film clip, a poem, a song, or a short commercial as the text for analysis. When assessing a mathematical concept, we can use a chart from popular culture or a graph from the news. When assessing fluency in a global language, we can ask students to compare the words and images used in headlines from different global newspapers. When assessing scientific knowledge, we can ask students to apply concepts from physics to the critique of a clip in an action movie. And when assessing historical knowledge, we can compare etchings, letters, maps, and paintings from the time period with contemporary messages about the same event from a TV show, a dramatic or documentary film, a website, or a video game.

The use of diverse media documents and formats in assessments serves a number of purposes. It gives students who are visual, auditory, and experiential learners, students who are more cued into diverse media, and students who have been alienated from traditional print forms access to showing their skills and knowledge. The use of diverse media in assessments—in particular, contemporary popular-culture texts—can engage students who may struggle with the relevancy of the curriculum. And the diversification of assessments can push us to incorporate diverse media more consistently into the curriculum, for as we know, tests often drive what and how we teach. But the use of diverse media alone does not integrate media literacy into assessments (or curriculum). Students also need to reflect on the constructed nature of media messages.

Pause to Reflect

How do you already assess critical-thinking skills (separate from knowledge and other skills) in your curriculum? How might you incorporate assessment of critical thinking about diverse media into your curriculum?

Some Models for Assessment

Merely using diverse media in tests does not ensure that the tests assess media literacy skills. We incorporate media literacy in our assessments when we ask questions that require students to demonstrate their ability to analyze, evaluate, and question media. This purpose can be achieved by using many different forms of media, by using different testing formats, and for assessing a range of different knowledge and skill outcomes. We will use the two paintings that we introduced in Chapter 3, *Discovery of the Mississippi* and *The Last Supper,* to illustrate different types of assessment questions using a media document (see Figure 6.1, pp. 112–113). Although the examples in the figure are for a hypothetical 11th grade history assessment, these types of questions can be applied to different subject areas and grade levels. For more detailed examples of different types of assessment questions using media analysis, search Project Look Sharp's lessons and filter your results by Student Activities and Assessments.

Multiple-choice questions. As shown in Figure 6.1, the format of multiple-choice questions can be particularly effective for a quick quantitative assessment of student knowledge of factual information. Additional approaches to short, quantitative, fact-based assessment include true/false and matching questions. Question #1 uses a media document to assess students' content knowledge. But multiple-choice questions can also be used to assess media literacy as well as subject-area vocabulary, knowledge, and concepts. In Question #2, students must reflect on the construction of the painting itself—what it "promotes"—to determine the right answer. To assess students' media analysis skills as well as content knowledge, it is useful to have a two-part question, such as Question #3.

Short-answer questions. As illustrated in Question #4 in Figure 6.1, short-answer questions allow us to assess knowledge and critical-thinking skills that are more complex while still being easily quantifiable and brief. They depend less on the student's writing ability than do longer essay questions, so they are good for targeting conceptual understandings. Answers earn points through reasonable evidence-based responses with explanations. Although students could give evidence for either perspective, reasonable evidence-based responses make it more likely for students to receive full credit for explanations of how the painting reflects a European perspective. Developing a simple rubric is useful in scoring short-answer questions.

Short-answer and essay questions. Figure 6.1 includes examples of short-answer and essay questions that are used regularly in social studies but can be adapted to assessments in any content area. Using a combination of short-answer questions leading up to an essay allows us to assess both conceptual understanding and students' abilities to integrate concepts with evidence into cohesive interpretations tied to a thesis (in the essay). Complex essay questions typically require students to interconnect different understandings from the curriculum with specific media texts as they choose appropriate evidence to illustrate their synthesis. Although the essay format is highly dependent on student writing skills (and comfort level), it can be modified to enable students to present orally (to a teacher or an aide) or through technology so that assessments of students' knowledge and conceptual understanding are separate from assessment of their ability to write an essay. Essay questions are more difficult to quantify, but a rubric can help ensure consistent scoring.

Performance-based assessments. Approaches to assessment such as the New York State Performance-Based Assessment Tasks (PBATs) are gaining favor nationally as an alternative to standardized testing (New York Performance Standards Consortium, 2020). They involve more authentic demonstrations of learning, often through interactions with experts in the field. An example would be to have a student complete an extensive research project on the change in national perspectives about first contact of Native Peoples and Europeans through the evolution of U.S. media representations over the last 200-plus years. The student would then give a brief presentation of their research (including media documents) and respond to questions by evaluators who would use a common rubric for assessment. Adding a student audience to this type of assessment can strengthen student scholarship and motivation.

FIGURE 6.1 **Examples of Assessment Questions**

Discovery of the Mississippi, William Powell, 1855

The Last Supper, Jonathan Warm Day, 1991

1. The central figure in the painting on the left was...

(a) a Spanish explorer   (b) an Italian conquistador   (c) an American settler

2. That painting, commissioned by Congress in 1847 to hang in the Rotunda of the U.S. Capitol, promotes which of the following?

(a) manifest destiny   (b) nativist pacifism   (c) Indigenous sovereignty

3. Hernando de Soto, the central figure in that painting, is portrayed as being...

(a) powerful   (b) subservient   (c) empathetic

Give three pieces of evidence from the painting to back up your answer. Evidence could include specific people or objects in the painting; use of color, line, angle, or space; body language of subjects; etc.

Evidence #1: _____.

Evidence #2: _____.

Evidence #3: _____.

4. Write a paragraph in the space below in which you...
   - Identify the painting as representing either a European or a Native American perspective.
   - Discuss three different aspects of the painting's construction that communicate that point of view.
   - Briefly explain for each aspect how that aspect communicates the perspective.

5. Write an essay using the two paintings, *Discovery of the Mississippi* painted in 1855 by William Henry Powell and *The Last Supper* painted in 1991 by Jonathan Warm Day, and using your knowledge of first contact between Native Peoples and Europeans. In your essay:

- Contrast the views of first contact presented in each painting.
- Discuss the historical context of each painting and how it reflects the views of the time period in which it was painted.
- Explain how changes in U.S. public perspectives on first contact changed from the 1850s to the 1990s.
- Use evidence from each painting to explain your analysis.

Source: Discovery of the Mississippi, Library of Congress. Public domain.
The Last Supper, © Jonathan Warm Day. Reproduced with permission.

Pre- and post-unit assessments. Another strategy for assessing student knowledge is to use the media document as a pre- and post-unit assessment of student learning. The 1st grade science lesson presented at the beginning of Chapter 1 is an example of this approach. Before the teacher began her unit on matter—liquid, solid, and gas—she showed her students the short clip from the cartoon video *Spider-Man vs. Hydro-Man* and asked, "What was true and not true about liquids in this short video clip?" At the end of the unit, when students had the background knowledge to give scientifically informed responses, she asked the same question. Priming students with the initial question at the beginning of the unit activated their "Velcro buds," and, for certain students, their learning about matter had more to stick to. (See the lesson *Liquids in Spider-Man vs. Hydro-Man* on the Project Look Sharp website, https://projectlooksharp.org/spiderman.)

Annotated bibliographies. When doing research projects that involve gathering information from multiple sources, students should be conscious of the biases of their sources as well as the sources' utility and credibility. These factors can be assessed by requiring an annotated bibliography, as illustrated in Figure 6.2. This example was designed for a 10th grade global studies research project that will be explained in Chapter

7. This format can be adapted to different grade levels and subjects. The expectations about the level of detail and analysis within the annotations will need to be simpler for earlier grades and more sophisticated for college students. Adapted for different levels and content, the bibliography requires students to reflect on each source's utility, given the particular goals of the research; its credibility for that specific topic; and any point of view or bias it may reflect.

FIGURE 6.2 Annotated Bibliography— Example for a Secondary Research Paper

Your bibliography should use our **standard citation format** followed by *annotations* (notes) on the **usefulness** of the source (why and how you might use it), its **credibility** (why you should trust it or not), and its **bias** (point of view).

Examples
Book:
Swart, Joan. *In Defense of Syria: The Speeches of Bashar al Assad.* Nook Books, 2012, print.
Usefulness—32 speeches by Assad, dated but good for his point of view.
Credibility/Bias—published by well-known bookseller, Barnes and Noble, all Assad's words.

Website:
The Arab Republic of Egypt Presidency, https://www.presidency.eg/en, April 20, 2021, web.
Usefulness—government views on lots of issues, including current *News,* updated daily.
Credibility/Bias—official website for President El-Sisi.

Newspaper or Magazine Article:
Ryan, Missy, and DeYoung, Karen. "Biden will withdraw all U.S. forces from Afghanistan by Sept. 11, 2021," the *Washington Post,* April 13, 2021, p. 32, print.
Usefulness—brief overview of Biden's policy and plan with concise background history.
Credibility/Bias—major newspaper, mainstream U.S. perspective.

Encyclopedia Article (or well-known reference books):
Encyclopedia Britannica, "Palestine Liberation Organization," 2020, print.
Usefulness—overview of PLO with lots of historical background up to 2020.
Credibility/Bias—unknown authors but reputable U.S. "encyclopedia" with
source references.

Online Newspaper or Magazine Article:
Bergman, Ronen, and Mazzetti, Mark. "The Secret History of the Push to
Strike Iran," *New York Times Magazine*, April 6, 2021, https://www.nytimes.
com/2019/09/04/magazine/iran-strike-israel-america.html
Usefulness—in-depth info on Israel's push for the U.S. to attack Iran over
nuclear conflict.
Credibility/Bias—major U.S. newspaper, considered "the standard" for good
journalism.

Online Podcast:
Zinn, Howard. "War and Social Justice," *Democracy Now: The War
and Peace Report*, Jan. 2, 2009, www.democracynow.org/2009/1/2/
placeholder_howard_zinn
Usefulness—30 minutes, good facts on how the Iraq War was manipulated by
the U.S. government.
Credibility/Bias—anti-Bush view, Zinn is a historian, *Democracy Now* is "progressive" news.

Source: © 2021 Chris Sperry. Used with permission.

Teaching Metacognition

In Chapter 1, we referenced a study by Kahne and Bowyer (2017) that
identified metacognition—the awareness and ability to reflect on our own
thought processes—as a critical element for students' capacity to evaluate truth claims. Their research showed that merely presenting students
with "the facts" is not enough (and probably never has been). In this time
of unlimited access to mediated statements of fact (many inaccurate)
to back up any claim, we need students to habitually reflect on their own
biases that might lead them to accept certain false claims. Students need
to be taught the concept of confirmation bias. They need to understand
that we tend to think more critically when confronted with information

that challenges our biases but accept information at face value when we see, hear, or read ideas that confirm what we believe. When students get in the habit of regularly reflecting on their own biases and the strengths and weaknesses of their own critical thinking, they become more skilled at assessing truth.

Schools can and need to play a critical role in the process of epistemological education. In addition to presenting essential facts and having students evaluate conflicting perspectives and provide evidence to back up their own judgments, we need to teach them to reflect on their own thinking. This lesson cannot be a one-time event—no matter how excellent. It requires consistent practice across disciplines and throughout the grades. CMD can provide an ideal opportunity to teach metacognition across the curriculum.

If every teacher would ask students to respond to versions of the following set of questions, phrased at the appropriate developmental level and applied to the subjects and documents taught, then we would have a truly metacognitive generation capable of better assessing truth claims:

- What are my intellectual and emotional reactions to this message?
- How do I evaluate the truth, credibility, and accuracy of these claims?
- How might my biases influence my interpretations, what I remember, and what I choose to share?
- How might others evaluate this differently, and why?
- What aspects of my life experience and identity influence my interpretations? How might my age, gender, race, family, religion, hometown, school, sexual orientation, or a host of other factors affect my interpretation?
- What do I learn about myself from my reactions or judgments?

There are many other versions of these questions, and they should look quite different in different contexts. For a 1st grade lesson on nutrition, for example, a teacher might ask: "Which of these cereal boxes looks the most fun?" "Why do you think so? Does everyone agree?" "Why do you think that different students picked different boxes?" In a middle school math class analyzing conflicting statistics about their own school, a teacher could ask: "Which of these charts seems most credible, and why?" "How might you answer differently if the charts were about another school?" "What might that say about how we assess the credibility of information?" In a high school health class that decodes two short videos about sexual harassment in social media, a teacher might ask: "Which of these videos do you relate to more?" "Which is more believable?" "Do we see any gendered patterns in the class's reactions to these videos? Why might that be?"

All these questions ask students to practice thinking about their own reactions, judgments, and thinking; to relate their thinking to the perspectives of others; and to begin to understand the complexities of knowledge. They also give students continual practice in inquiry—in asking questions. Because the ability to inquire is an essential skill, we need to be teaching our students how to ask good questions.

Having Students Ask the Questions and Lead the Decoding

So far we have been focusing on having the teacher ask the questions when leading the decoding. With experience in classroom media analysis, students can become quite adept at the decoding process and can be expected to ask their own questions and ultimately to lead the decoding themselves. One simple way to get students to begin asking good questions about any media document is to ask them the following: "What question(s) should we be asking about this?" You could have students lead a decoding activity in small groups, online, or even for the whole class.

When Chris started asking his high school students to generate their own questions, he noticed that it was a real struggle for some students, including some of the most academically capable students. One student suggested that school was about answering questions, not asking them. It was not until Chris started to hold students accountable for asking questions (on quizzes) that all students began to take it seriously.

With the expectation that they had to ask questions themselves, his students started to practice developing questions. Over time, their questions began to reflect patterns. Some students tended to ask only concrete questions ("Where was that picture taken?"). Other students gravitated toward questions of moral judgment ("Is globalized media a good or bad thing?"). And other students always asked big philosophical questions ("Is humanity doomed?"). Chris began to reflect on the different types of questions that different students tended to ask, and you can do the same thing with your students. This effort is likely to improve the quality and diversity of their questions as the students think more about them. Although students may typically ask media decoding questions that you model (e.g., from the Key Questions handout, shown in Figure 3.2, p. 44), they may also come up with original questions reflecting their insight and creativity.

With practice in developing questions about media coupled with experience in teacher-led media decoding, students are often ready to jump into leading the decoding process themselves. They will need to think through how hard or easy the question will be for their peers and what background information, if any, the class will need to respond to a question. By asking the student decoding leaders to think through how the class might respond to their specific questions, they will begin to think like a teacher. This shift will come quite naturally for some students, and they may not only come up with terrific questions but also do a great job leading the analysis. As one elementary teacher commented, "Kevin—a typically quiet, disaffected student—led an awesome decoding."

Assessing Questioning and Metacognition

If we are serious about the importance of having students ask good, thoughtful questions and reflect on their own thinking, we need to test them on their abilities to ask good questions and to reflect on their own biases. What would an assessment look like that tests questioning and metacognition? As with all assessments, it is most critical that we actually assess the specific knowledge and abilities that we are targeting. In too many tests, we are unintentionally assessing students' cultural backgrounds, their comfort or anxiety with test taking, their familiarity with the particular formats in the test, or their capabilities related to the testing format (e.g., essay writing). We should take these concerns into consideration as we integrate media analysis, questioning strategies, and metacognition into our assessments.

Figure 6.3 shows one example of an assessment developed for high school students that tests their critical thinking about media messages, their ability to ask questions, and their thinking about their own thinking. It was developed by the staff at the Lehman Alternative Community School in 2015 to assess the school's progress in teaching critical-thinking skills. It was delivered to all 9th through 12th grade students during their English classes and took about 30 minutes. It intentionally integrated science content about a controversial issue (genetically modified organisms, or GMOs) with the kind of media analysis typically done in humanities classes. The test asked students to analyze a variety of media texts: a short YouTube video, an excerpt from a print article, and a screen grab from a website. It presents a model for a relatively short, multigrade summative assessment of critical-thinking skills. The test assesses students' abilities to do the following:

- Identify the bias in media texts about a controversial issue.
- Provide appropriate evidence from documents to back up their interpretations.
- Connect an author's purpose with the choices made in constructing a text.
- Ask appropriate questions about the credibility of sources.
- Reflect on their own biases and how those might affect their evaluation of the credibility of different sources.

These objectives can be adapted and applied to assessing students' media analysis skills at different levels, about different content, using different media documents.

FIGURE 6.3 **Example of an Assessment of Critical-Thinking Skills**

You are going to look at three different media documents about genetically modified foods (GMOs):

- A three-minute YouTube video, *Genetic Engineering: The World's Greatest Scam*
- An excerpt from a *New York Times* op-ed piece, "How I Got Converted to GMO Food"
- A screen grab from a website, *Genetically Engineered Food*

You will have 10 minutes to read the article and the website screen grab before we show you the video. First read the questions below.

1. The position of the video is best described as . . . (Circle the best answer below.)

(a) pro-GMO   (b) anti-GMO   (c) neutral

2. Describe three specific choices made by the filmmakers that helped them to communicate their position on GMOs (e.g., the use of particular music, imagery, facts, etc.). For each choice, explain how it communicated that position.

Choice #1 and how it communicates the position on GMOs:

_____

Choice #2 and how it communicates the position on GMOs:

_____

Choice #3 and how it communicates the position on GMOs:

_____

3. The point of view or bias of the video reflects the mission of the organization that paid for/produced it. Below are the mission statements for three different organizations. For each organization, indicate if it is likely to have produced the video (check Yes, No, or Unclear). Give a short explanation of your reasoning in the space provided.

Monsanto: We are a sustainable agriculture company. We deliver agricultural products that support farmers all around the world. We produce in-the-seed trait technologies for farmers, which are aimed at protecting their yield, supporting their on-farm efficiency, and reducing their on-farm costs.

Yes ☐   No ☐   Unclear ☐

Explanation: _____

Greenpeace: We are the largest independent direct-action environmental organization in the world. We defend the natural world and promote peace by investigating, exposing, and confronting environmental abuse, championing environmentally responsible solutions, and advocating for the rights and well-being of all people.

Yes ☐   No ☐   Unclear ☐

Explanation: _____

The Cornell Alliance for Science: We seek to promote access to scientific innovation as a means of enhancing food security, improving environmental sustainability, and raising the quality of life globally.

Yes ☐   No ☐   Unclear ☐

Explanation: _____

4. The word *credibility* is defined as "the quality of being trusted or believable." Write three important questions you would want answered in assessing the credibility of one or more of these documents.

Question #1: _____

_____

Question #2: _____

_____

Question #3: _____

_____

Which of the three documents most reflects your views on genetically modified organisms? (Circle one.)

The video   The op-ed   The website

5. Explain how your views on the issue of GMOs might influence how you understand and interpret these documents.

_____

_____

_____

_____

Assessment and Citizenship

There are many different approaches to assessing students' abilities to ask questions, including some being developed at a national level to test how students assess credibility as they search the internet. It will be a great advance to standardized testing if and when high-stakes tests such as the SATs require students to show that they know how to ask essential questions about credibility and bias when searching for information. And we will have a truly media-literate populace when our most important assessments test students' abilities to reflect on their own thinking. In the meantime, we can model these kinds of assessments in our in-class tests and quizzes, at whatever level and for whatever subject we teach. Doing so will certainly drive us to make sure that we integrate those skills and habits into our teaching.

The first two decades of the 21st century have highlighted the need for students to become better critical thinkers about the information presented to them and about their own meaning making related to those messages. The events of the last decade have made it clear that we cannot rely on "the facts" to lead them to "the truth." Our new media ecology is inundated with all the "facts" necessary to "prove" both accurate and inaccurate ideas and to reinforce biased, narrow, and simplistic views. If we are to prepare the next generation with the critical-thinking skills necessary to negotiate a perpetually polarized, politicized, and propagandized information environment, we need to incorporate these critical questioning skills throughout the curriculum and teach them at all levels and in diverse disciplines; we need students to continually practice, practice, practice media analysis, evaluation, and self-reflection. This goal will become a reality when our assessments test these essential abilities.

PEDAGOGICAL CONNECTIONS
AND INSPIRATIONS

The media literacy methodology presented in this book intersects with many different pedagogical approaches, educational initiatives, and classroom practices, and constructivist media decoding has been informed by many different disciplines. As we have stated earlier, the field of media literacy is the foundational discipline underlying CMD. But the CMD approach has also been shaped in critical ways by other educational initiatives.

The backward-planning approach to curriculum design known as Understanding by Design (UBD) (Wiggins & McTighe, 2005) has helped to shape Project Look Sharp's commitment to always grounding decoding in our goals, and the recent focus on standards has helped to target that work. Interdisciplinary education helps us to embrace the interconnected nature of literacy as it applies to all content areas and grade levels, and the pedagogy of holistic education keeps us focused on educating the whole child rather than teaching subjects. As explored in Chapter 3, developmental psychology underlies our approach to constructivism and keeps our attention on students' meaning making.

In this chapter, we will explore the place of CMD in other classroom methodologies and pedagogies, including media production, performance- and project-based learning (PBL), social-emotional learning (SEL), cultural competency, and antiracist education.

CMD Coupled with Media Production

It is important to note that constructivist media decoding, with its focus on analysis and evaluation, by itself does not address all aspects of media literacy education (see Figure 2.1, The Media Literacy Process, p. 26). Although media creation is not the focus of this book, we believe that student media production brings creativity, synthesis, and action to the analysis and evaluation of media. And the CMD process can be a critical component of any media production work by students. Although the creation of media messages by students does not require media decoding—and conversely, CMD does not necessitate production—the integration of both is a powerful combination that deepens the potential impact on students' lifelong learning. As with traditional print media, we want our students to be thoughtful, skilled, and responsible writers as well as readers, to be literate citizens involved in both well-reasoned thinking about their worlds and responsible participation in creating their worlds.

Inquiry and reflection should be at the center of all components of media literacy, including in student media production. CMD brings reflection on both technical and ethical considerations into the production process. When students who are producing media reflect on the choices they make as creators, they become more adept at analyzing the choices made in mass media production. When they use the CMD process to analyze and evaluate the techniques of media production and the varied interpretations and effects of mass media messages, they become more attuned to the important choices they make when creating media themselves.

One of the six key concepts in media analysis (described in Chapter 2) is that *each medium has different characteristics, strengths, and a unique "language" of construction.* This concept is especially important for students to internalize in this age of new media. We as educators must help students to grapple with the qualities and limitations of the media forms that are having dramatic effects on their lives and on society. Social media such as YouTube, Facebook, and Twitter have played a critical role in our current political and social polarization. The economic incentives that drive the algorithms that in turn drive online virality have propelled our epistemological crisis. For the next generation of students to have agency in a hypermediated world, they need to be able to continually reflect on the motivations, qualities, and particularities of the media that dominate our culture. The technologies and platforms will change over time, but the need for citizens to continually analyze and evaluate the media and their impacts will remain a constant. There is no better way for students to internalize an understanding of the uniqueness of different media forms than to become creators in different media. CMD can play a critical role in facilitating the analytical practices necessary for that learning.

In preparation for creating a print public service announcement, a short video, a poster, a short story, or any type or genre of media message, students will gain important production skills as they practice critiquing media messages that use that form. This exercise can even be done with things such as slide presentations. Having students analyze and critique PowerPoint creations that have problems with color choices, fonts, too much text, misspellings, and so forth can improve their own skills beyond just providing a list of do's and don'ts. Taking the time in class to have students collectively analyze different examples of the media they will be producing builds the technical skills for effective expression and communication. By asking questions about the construction of mass media messages ("What techniques did they use, and why?"), the CMD process can teach production skills through student-centered learning. It also models the kinds of questions students should ask about their own productions, such as "Who is my target audience?" "What information will I include, and how do I know it is accurate?" "Whose voices will I highlight, and whose will I leave out?" "Who might benefit from my message, and who might be harmed by it?" and "How might different people interpret my message differently?"

Media Production and Analysis— An Elementary Example

In our experience, it is elementary educators—particularly early-elementary teachers—who regularly say that they *need* to incorporate media production into any media literacy unit. Despite the fact that media production is complex and interdisciplinary, requiring more sophisticated technical skills and expertise than purely analytical work, it is the early-elementary teachers who push to integrate student-led, hands-on media creation into their lessons. Perhaps secondary educators could learn a bit from these colleagues about the motivating factor that action can play in learning.

As an example of the integration of CMD and media production, 2nd grade students at Caroline Elementary School in Ithaca, New York, were given the task of creating documentary videos as the final project for their environmental science/ELA unit on watersheds and threats to water systems. The teachers based their unit on Project Look Sharp lessons in the curriculum kit *Media Constructions of Sustainability: Lower Elementary* (https://projectlooksharp.org/sustainabilitylowerelem). They led a series of CMD activities critiquing advertisements and videos created by other elementary school students. After watching a short model video in its entirety, the class then went through the video again, pausing at key points to ask questions about the techniques used and their effectiveness. This process helped the students both to conceptualize possible approaches to their films and to identify specific video production elements and techniques for their particular purpose and audience. With help from the teachers and the technology support staff, the students worked in small groups to write scripts and "shot sheets" for different sections of the video. Although the teachers did the final editing of the documentary films, the students were involved in the decision making about what content to include or leave out, the order of the scenes, and the framing of the "story" they were telling.

Like most media production lessons, this 2nd grade project is a good example of truly interdisciplinary learning. The media production activity in particular taught a range of diverse skills aligned to ELA, social studies, and science standards, as well as many "soft skills." The unit taught ELA skills in *Reading* diverse texts (print, video, audio), *Writing* in multiple forms (scripts, shot sheets, and audio/video production), and *Speaking and Listening* (through multiple and diverse modes) (Common Core State Standards Initiative, 2021). As our own experiences attest, this multimodal approach to literacy can help students who are challenged by print literacy to develop critical skills and experience that they can then apply to mastering printed text. College, Career, and Civic Life (C-3) Social Studies Standards addressed by the 2nd grade production lessons include skills in *Participation and Deliberation* (group work, values clarification, etc.) and *Communicating Conclusions and Taking Informed Action* (using print, oral, and digital technologies) (National Council for the Social Studies, 2021).

The focus of the research and student videos produced by the Caroline 2nd graders also aligned with a number of Next Generation Science Standards for specific content understandings. To see specific standards addressed in these elementary lessons on video production, as well as the student handouts and media materials, review the kits *Media Production of Sustainability: Lower Elementary* (https://projectlooksharp.org/sustainabilitylowerelem) and *Media Production of Sustainability: Upper Elementary* (https://projectlooksharp.org/sustainabilityupperelem) on the Project Look Sharp website. In those kits you will also see other lessons that combine analysis and production using different media forms, including social media and postcards.

When students are asked to publicly demonstrate their understanding of ideas—for instance, communicating in video about local environmental issues—their learning is grounded in performance. For many students, this approach can be a key motivating force for learning. The CMD activities, the scientific knowledge taught in class, their research, the scripts and shot sheets, the technical tools of media production, and the group work and decision making all culminate in a public exhibition of skills and knowledge. The 2nd grade Caroline students shared their final videos about the endangered watershed surrounding their school through an evening "red carpet" event for parents, administrators, community members, and the press. This authentic audience helped to drive impressive scholarship and effort, but it also motivated students to do the deep self-reflection that characterizes effective media literacy. Five months later, in a follow-up assessment by an outside evaluator, students recalled the details of the information they had learned about water pollution and sustainable practices and were enthusiastic about having influenced others with their videos. One girl said excitedly, "My older brother stopped throwing litter on the ground after he saw my movie! He hadn't thought about it before!"

Combining CMD with media production leverages the deep motivation, personal investment, and empowerment that help to facilitate lifelong learning for a broad range of students. The kind of integrated, interdisciplinary, interactive learning that comes with complex media production activities also bears many of the hallmarks of project-based learning (Condliffe et al., 2017). It involves individual and collective work and decision making about real-world issues. It involves research, communication skills, and an iterative process of building toward a more complex understanding of an authentic problem. It is fundamentally interdisciplinary while being tied to the core principles of literacy—teaching students to both read and write about their worlds.

CMD and Project-Based Learning—Two Case Studies

Constructivist media decoding can be a critical tool in the curriculum of a deep PBL curriculum. As examples, we will look at two project-based learning units—one for middle school and the other (developed long before the term *project-based learning* was codified) for high school—and how media decoding played a key role in their development and success.

A Middle School Presentation on Ancient Rome

In the spring of 2017, nearly 100 students in the 6th grade class at Boynton Middle School in Ithaca, New York, gave an evening presentation to family and community members on their projects about ancient Rome. The demonstrations included papers about Roman leaders, sports, education, technology, gender, family life, science, medicine, government, religion, architecture, and economics. The evening also included interactive student presentations about Roman recreation, entertainment, engineering, and gladiators.

Although the projects tied to different academic disciplines, the overarching theme was *How do we know what we know about Rome?* Nearly the entire 6th grade team of educators participated in the planning and instruction through science, math, art, physical education, special education, ELA, social studies, and library studies classes. The teachers developed and taught new units integrating aspects of ancient Rome into their core curriculum, all tying to the theme of *How we know what we know*.

In social studies and in the library curriculum, this undertaking included a close examination of the divergent views about Julius Caesar, with an evaluation of the bias of the sources. In STEM, students examined the engineering of aqueducts and the development of medicine, continually reflecting on the accuracy and credibility of their sources. In art, students compared different depictions of the same events, questioning the works' historical accuracy while analyzing the technical choices of the painters. And in physical education, students analyzed film clips and video games showing gladiator events and then simulated chariot races in the gym to study techniques, develop physical abilities, and have fun.

In all of these curriculum-driven lessons, students continually reflected on how they know (or don't know) what they know. The CMD process can be instrumental in teaching practical academic skills that are the building blocks for the epistemological epiphanies described in the next example.

A High School Unit on the Middle East

In 1986, Chris had the opportunity to develop a new component for his high school humanities class that integrated core English and global studies requirements for 10th graders. As developed, the nine-week unit on the Middle East begins with each student taking on the role of a leader from a nation or group involved in regional politics, including the heads of state of many Middle Eastern nations, as well as the United States and Russia, opposition groups, militant organizations, and human rights representatives. The unit culminates in a weeklong public performance of student learning through a simulated conference, including more than three hours of debate on a host of issues. The students are evaluated on their ability to consistently and accurately reflect the perspective (cultural, national, religious, etc.) of their character through their use of language, facts, narrative, and voice. The development of that unit—which became a model for the school's performance-based assessments—is linked to the use and success of CMD.

The first year that Chris taught the Middle East unit, the debates were a bust. Students represented the characters by mimicking the stereotypes common to U.S. media coverage of the Middle East in the mid-1980s. Chris knew that he needed to help students to understand and represent the authentic voices of leaders from diverse Middle East nations and groups. Some of these leaders had fundamentalist religious views, some were considered terrorists by the West, and most were skilled politicians who chose their every word for its potential impact on different audiences. Working backward from these goals, Chris brought these perspectives to his students through eight weeks of media decoding activities, using the CMD process to teach core knowledge about the Middle East, and an understanding of how a careful use of words, stories, tone, voice, images, and information reflect an author's perspective, bias, and intent. In our experience, students find this approach to learning more engaging than just watching videos, reading texts, or listening to lectures. They developed the expectation that they would actively participate in analyzing all the texts for content and construction, perspectives, and biases. Figure 7.1 shows examples of just some of the Project Look Sharp lessons Chris created with his brother, Sox Sperry, that address these content and literacy goals. (For these lessons and more, see Project Look Sharp's kit *Media Construction of the Middle East* at https://projectlooksharp.org/middleeast.)

FIGURE 7.1 **Content and Media Documents for Lessons in a Unit on the Middle East**	
Core Content	**Media Documents Used for Decoding**
Stereotyping	Introduction to Disney's movie *Aladdin*, clips from U.S. TV shows
Islam	Muslim and U.S. encyclopedia articles*
U.S.–Iranian Relations	*Time* magazine covers from 1934 until the present
Iraq War	Front pages from international newspaper reporting on key events in the war
Israel/Palestine	Textbooks, websites, maps, and songs from Israeli and Palestinian sources
Arab Spring	Facebook posts, YouTube videos, comedy, music, art, and other media forms used in eight Arab nations to promote social change

* See Figure 3.1, Definitions of Islam, on page 42.

Throughout this unit, the students were doing their own independent research on the history and perspectives of their nations and characters, ultimately completing papers that ranged in length from 8 to more than 80 pages, with an average of 40 sources. Students needed to write their papers using first-person point of view to reflect the political, religious, and personal perspective of their character. Students also needed to complete an annotated bibliography identifying the utility, credibility, and bias of each source (topics that are discussed in Chapter 5; see also Figure 6.2, pp. 114–115, for a sample bibliography).

The Epistemological Curriculum

Throughout the Middle East unit, CMD enabled students to consistently reflect on their own thinking, their own valuing, their understanding of truth, and the constructed nature of knowledge. It meshed with the epistemological curriculum of adolescence as teenagers struggled to develop their own views. The words of the students themselves are the best illustrations of the impact of consistent integration of media decoding into the core social studies and ELA curricula. The following are excerpts from the self-evaluations of the 10th grade students at the end of the unit:

- "One of the most important aspects of this class for me was the fact that it not only made me stand by some of my beliefs, but it made me question others of my beliefs. Some of the views I have carried with me my whole life were questioned, not only by others, but by myself as well."
- "Through this course I have looked far into myself, questioned my morals and beliefs, and have begun to search for my place in history and my place in the world. I have now glimpsed how much there is to learn, and I am overwhelmed."
- "This class has taught me how to think, how to question. It taught me that everything has a bias, and to never accept anything as the only truth."
- "I have a newfound desire to learn as well as be aware of the world, how it is presented to me and how I perceive it. I feel better prepared for school as well as life in general."

One of the clear themes that emerges from these comments is the role that media literacy can play in helping adolescents to reflect on their own learning, their own valuing, their own meaning making. CMD activities can provoke students to rigorously analyze divergent narratives; to see, hear, and attempt to understand the voices of others, including their peers; to commit to their own point of view and back it up with evidence; and to reflect deeply on their own judgments, biases, and beliefs. Authentic reflection on the value of knowledge, the meaning of truth, and one's role in seeking both can and should be at the core of the adolescent curriculum.

The 2nd grade environmental media production unit, the schoolwide 6th grade Rome project, and the high school Middle East debates are all examples that show how CMD can be a key curricular methodology for learning experiences that are deeply engaging, student-centered, interdisciplinary, project-based, and inquiry-driven, and that culminate in public performances. All three are time-consuming but highly effective units that also teach important social skills and cultural competencies.

CMD and Social-Emotional Learning

The movement for SEL reminds us that the affective component of learning is critical to student success. For students—particularly those dealing with trauma and other emotional challenges—there is no real separation between the affective and the cognitive. Although we can look at SEL as a tool to deal with "problem students," it is more accurately and effectively approached as a lens through which to look at all our teaching and our curriculum. Are we supporting students in developing the key social-emotional skills they need for success in life and society? CMD can play a supportive role in helping students to learn and practice SEL skills and habits.

At the core of SEL are the competencies of self-awareness, self-management, responsible decision making, relationship building, and social awareness. Each of these can be practiced—and some taught directly—through a well-facilitated collective analysis of media messages. Students practice and learn self-awareness when they participate in a structured protocol of sharing different perspectives on provocative media messages. They become aware that, at times, their views are different from those of their peers. To quote one 10th grade student, "Media literacy has allowed me to kind of learn that I have my own opinions and that they're different in some cases from what the standard cultural norms are and that it's OK to have different opinions, and everyone has their own different ideas and they'll be again different from person to person."

The structure of CMD, with individual students sharing their evidence-based perspectives and then listening to others, models the kind of cognitive management that we aim to help develop in students and in society. It teaches them to share observations, interpretations, and judgments related to a text, to externalize their views and experiences onto a media document while listening to the views of others about the same message. This structured process of communicating one's ideas, sharing opinions, and reflecting on one's own experience provides a relatively safe protocol for self-management around potentially challenging topics.

By asking students to think about why their peers may interpret messages differently and to reflect on the sources of their own views, they are taught to be metacognitive, to think about their thinking and their emotional experience. Putting these concepts into words, describing the feelings and exploring the roots of one's affect is a key component of SEL. The process also teaches students to listen to the meaning making of their peers, to learn from each other, and to develop empathy. Successful CMD as a regular part of the class experience can help to develop the collegial bonds of shared intellectual and academic work that is critical to the ethos of trust and learning in a classroom. When we add media production, the opportunities for shared decision making and relationship building expand exponentially.

Integrating constructivist media decoding, social-emotional learning, project-based learning, and media production can lead to powerful, student-centered experiences that build school success for more students. And these approaches should not be decontextualized from the pervasive racial and cultural realities that dominate the lives of our students, particularly those most marginalized in their school experience (Madda, 2019).

CMD and Cultural Competency

CMD can be a great tool for listening to the cultural perspectives and diversity of students both for ourselves as teachers and for our students. When we hear students' varied interpretations of a media document, be it a 1st grader commenting on a photograph about family or a 12th grader reflecting on the reality of climate change, we are likely to be tapping into their cultural background and experience. By tuning in to not only the content of their interpretations but also the affective expressions in their body language, voice, and tone, we listen for important signals about their place in our classroom. When we watch closely the reactions of their peers to comments made during a decoding activity, we assess the underlying dynamics in the classroom. And as we notice and reflect on our own reactions to different students and their contributions during media analysis, we can develop self-awareness of our own cultural orientations and biases.

In the fall of 2007, Project Look Sharp and the Ithaca City School District planned to launch a collectively developed curriculum kit for 1st grade. The *All Our Families* project had begun more than a year earlier when we asked a group of more than 300 elementary teachers what new media literacy materials they needed for their curriculum. First grade teacher Randi Beckmann immediately stood and told this story. She had recently begun her family unit by placing a series of old black-and-white photos of families around the room. When the students went to lunch, one student stayed, walking back and forth in front of the photos before collapsing on the ground in tears. When Randi asked him what was wrong, he said, "My family is not here." This courageous and expressive 1st grader was African American and had two White moms. Randi immediately took the photos down and asked students to bring in photos of their own families. Months later, when we asked the question about resources, she immediately requested that we create a new set of photos that would reflect the broad diversity of all the families in the Ithaca City School District.

After a year of committee work—developing criteria, interviewing and photographing families, writing teacher guides, and planning professional development—we were ready to unveil our series of beautiful 14-by-20-inch photographs to the librarians who would be presenting this project to their 1st grade teachers (see Figure 7.2 , pp. 138–139). Each photo had a teacher guide on the back with the family story, key vocabulary, questions for media decoding with the 1st graders, extension activities, and additional resources. Every photo included a local 1st grade–age student with their family and showed activities that the family members said helped to make them a family.

During a workshop where we unveiled this new kit to the district's elementary librarians, we presented the photographs and gave them time to read through the lesson guides on the back of each. Almost immediately, two of the women broke off from the group and had a private conversation in the back of the room. They were the librarians from our two rural schools. They returned to the group and told us (somewhat apologetically), "I am afraid your work is not done. Many of the students in our schools live in mobile homes, in trailer parks. If their homes are ever presented in the media, it is in a derogatory way. You need to add one more photo to this collection." Another librarian added, "Many of our families are headed by a single mom. Where is she in these photos?" We immediately got to work and soon added an additional family photo card showing a young mom with her five elementary-age children and their dog, playing around their swing set in front of their mobile home.

This story illustrates what cultural competency can mean in the context of media literacy. It was not easy for the two librarians to ask us to change our timeline for rolling out the curriculum and get back to work adding another family. But their higher priority was the safety and inclusiveness of their classrooms. The librarians immediately recognized how the cultural identities of their children were not represented in the photos. Our important project would not have met its goals without their advocacy, their understanding of the meaning making of their students, and their cultural competency.

As we use the power of media to teach our students and bring diverse media representations into our classrooms for analysis, critique, and appreciation, we need to be continually mindful of the power of media to teach, to harm, and to empower. Although first and foremost we must do no harm in our use of media in the classroom, we also have the responsibility to use the power of media to redress harms and to teach our students to have agency with the media that inundate their lives. The most important tools in this struggle are our abilities to listen well to our students, to always keep our "Velcro buds" active to the question of cultural interpretations and influences, and to be humble in our role as educators. We will make mistakes, and our families know that. But we need to be open to our own limitations while always striving to become better listeners, better learners, and better advocates for identities that are not necessarily our own.

Paulo Freire and Antiracist Education

Although the movement for antiracist education has gained greater visibility in response to the Black Lives Matter movement, its history lies in the civil rights movement of the 1960s, the movements to abolish slavery and challenge Jim Crow, and the struggles of Black people in the Americas for more than 500 years. It is grounded in the understanding that culture and identity are not neutral in any society. Systems that privilege particular groups and marginalize others typically have deep and entrenched roots that are not simple to unearth.

In the case of the United States, this system goes back to the founding economic institution of race-based slavery. The branches of this ancient organization spread across all aspects of our society, including and especially education. Our schools, classrooms, and teaching inevitably reflect these foundational structures. To ignore the power of this history and of these systems, to claim to be color blind, is not to be neutral but to side with the status quo. Antiracist education calls on us to examine the systems within our classrooms, schools, and educational structures that perpetuate White supremacy. This lens can be applied to our work in media decoding as we look at the role of the teacher and the media messages we bring into our curriculum.

FIGURE 7.2 **Photos and Lesson Plan for the *All Our Families* Curriculum Kit**

THE MENDEZ FAMILY

Project Look Sharp
ITHACA COLLEGE

Key Vocabulary

immigration, Mexican-American, library, Vietnamese

Initial Questions

(See Teacher's Guide)

What do you see in this picture?

What do you notice about this family?

What would you like to know about this family?

Family Story

The Mendez family has lived in Ithaca for 2 years. Before that they lived in Albuquerque, New Mexico, where all 3 children were born. Thu and Sergio met in college in California.

Some of the family's favorite activities are to read and swim together. They have no extended family in Ithaca. They occasionally visit their relatives in California.

Last Names (Optional)

When Thu married Sergio, she took his last name, Mendez. All three children also have the last name Mendez.

Notes to Teacher

Mendez Notes: Many 5- and 6-year-olds do not recognize race as an identifying feature. They may not see that mom is Vietnamese and dad is Mexican-American. Tell them these facts, but allow them to disregard this as unimportant.

Follow-Up Questions

Do you think the Mendez family likes going to the library?

Why do you think that?

Do you think the children see their grandparents often?

Why do you think that?

How do you think they feel about that?

Do you have members of your family that you do not see very often?

Alyson Mendez – 7 years old. Likes to draw and play make-believe games.

Sergio Mendez – 37 years old. Was born and grew up in Southern California. His parents still live in California. Has brothers and sisters in the U.S. and in Mexico. He is a 4th generation Mexican-American. Married to Thu.

Dante Mendez – 2 years old. Loves to be like his older brother.

Thu Mendez – 34 years old. Was born and lived in Vietnam until she was 18 years old. Came to the U.S. in 1989. Has a sister and brother who both live in the U.S. Stay-at-home mom. Volunteers at her children's school. Married to Sergio.

Bernard Mendez – 5 years old. He likes arts and crafts.

Extension Activities/Questions

What questions would you ask the children in this family?

Find the different places mentioned in the family story on a map.

Discuss the phrase: "4th generation Mexican-American"

How do the family members look the same/different from each other?

What do you like to do with your family?

Children's Books

- Garland, Sherry. *Children of the Dragon: Selected Tales from Vietnam*, Harcourt, 2001.
- Namioka, Lensey. *Half and Half*, Delacorte Books for Young Readers, 2003.
- Hoyt-Goldsmith, Diane. *Hoang Anh: A Vietnamese- American Boy*, Harcourt Brace & Company, 1997.
- Viesti, Joseph and Diane Hall. *Celebrate! in Southeast Asia*, William Morrow & Co. Library, 1996.

Photo by Peter Ozolins

The National Museum of African American History and Culture (2021) defines antiracist education as follows:

> A theory of learning and action to help us do the important work of dismantling racism in schools. It explicitly highlights, critiques, and challenges institutional racism. It addresses how racist beliefs and ideologies structure one-on-one interactions and personal relationships. It also examines and challenges how institutions support and maintain disadvantages and advantages along racial lines.

Our classrooms are microcosms of society, either perpetuating or transforming the traditional power structures, values, and actions of the larger systems. If we are to challenge the caste structures that perpetuate racial, class, and gendered hierarchies, we need to scrutinize and transform our role as teachers.

Paulo Freire (1970) described the "banking method" of education, in which the teacher "makes deposits which the students patiently receive, memorize and repeat" (p. 58). This pedagogy sees students as empty vessels to be filled with knowledge. Freire contrasted that with education for liberation, in which the teacher facilitates a process of critical reflection based on life experience, with students developing their awareness of the forces in society that are holding them back from being more fully human. Freire's work with illiterate peasants in Brazil in the 1960s—like the CMD process—shifts the power dynamic between teacher and student. In this approach to literacy, the teacher leads a collective process that empowers students to think critically, to analyze and evaluate codes of social meaning, to listen to the views of their peers, and to reflect on their own thinking. The ultimate goal of Freire's process of "conscientization" is a praxis of thought and action.

Ibram X. Kendi, author of *How to Be an Antiracist* (2019), states that "the only way to undo racism is to consistently identify it and describe it—and then dismantle it" (p. 9). Like Freire, Kendi names the bringing together of awareness, language, and action as core to changing the world. Antiracist education uses reflection, history, and an awareness of power to make changes to deeply entrenched historical systems of privilege and oppression. For teachers, this awareness includes reflection on our own identities and the implicit biases that do disservice to children of color. This educational shift challenges the traditional privileges of the teacher and calls for new ways of teaching that bring forward the voices and needs of students, particularly historically marginalized populations. Antiracist education sees Black people as core agents in the history of the United States and confronts the role of racism in perpetuating White supremacy as a cornerstone in the oppressive structures that have held the nation back from keeping its promises.

So how does this relate to constructivist media decoding? The shift in the role of the teacher in the CMD process fundamentally challenges a banking pedagogy. As teachers, we must work with the constructed nature of students' understanding of the world. In facilitating the collective organisms that are our classrooms, we lead students toward greater complexity in their thinking, greater compassion and empathy, greater curiosity, and more reflective action. At the center of this shift is the ability to hear the meaning making of our students—in particular, the students who have been historically alienated from the mechanism of schooling. In U.S. society, this shift will inevitably require a focus of attention on Black students, families, and lives that have been systematically suppressed in our educational systems, schools, and classrooms, and in the minds of teachers.

On a practical level, applying antiracist education to the CMD process necessitates reflection on how the privileging of Whiteness lives in our schools, classrooms, and teaching. It calls on us to be vigilant in our self-reflection about who we call on in the decoding process, who we privilege with attention, who we let remain silent, who we ask to elaborate on their comments, who we cut off, and who we challenge. Antiracist CMD asks that we be accountable for our own implicit biases—not with guilt and shame, but with a commitment to continually unearth those biases with humility and the determination to effectively challenge them.

Antiracist CMD requires us to be aware of the power dynamics in the classroom. In shifting our role from banker to facilitator, we do not give up power but shift the focus and intent of that power. We hold responsibility for what happens in the classroom, for providing safety, and for meeting learning objectives. We structure the classroom, set the agenda, and frame the activity. We choose the media documents, ask the questions, and lead the decoding; but it is the students' thinking and feeling, their meaning making, that provide the content for the decoding.

When dealing with challenging issues such as race, class, gender, and other identity-related issues, we need to be particularly conscious of the spoken and unspoken dynamics in our classrooms and their impact on students and on classroom life. Being student-centered does not mean that we abdicate responsibility for leading our classroom. On the contrary, it requires that we manage classroom dynamics to create trust, safety, and deep learning, or as Freire describes, empathic dialogue (Freire & Macedo, 1998). This undertaking requires not only discernment in what media and issues we bring into our classrooms but also courage in addressing the systemic issues that underlie the nation's founding sins.

Representations of Race

We need to examine the media we celebrate (e.g., post on our walls) as well as the media we decode. It is important to have positive images of people of color in our lessons, to have media messages about African Americans who have achieved success nationally and globally, and to celebrate different aspects of cultural diversity. It is important to advance in our curriculum the voices of Black people and other people of color who have challenged the structures of White supremacy in the United States. The following Project Look Sharp lessons can serve as models for media decoding activities that do just that:

- The lesson *Arguing for Freedom* (https://projectlooksharp.org/freedom) includes newspaper articles, engravings, posters, a book cover, and other 19th century media documents (created by African Americans) about slavery and abolition.

- *Youth Activism* (https://projectlooksharp.org/youthactivism) has students decode four short video clips that advance the voices of Black activists in the 1960s.
- The lesson *Harriet Tubman Seizes Freedom—Many Stories* (https://projectlooksharp.org/harriettubmanfreedom) has elementary-age students decode different book excerpts about the well-known abolitionist for messages about slavery and the Underground Railroad.

In addition to promoting images and stories that give voice to the Black experience in the United States, we also need to teach students to understand forces of structural inequity. It is important to expose them to media that bring appropriate moral emotion to the nation's history of racial oppression. But messages about the victimization and suffering of "poor non-Whites" also risk perpetuating stereotypical thinking. We should aim to present and analyze representations that witness the depth of experience, explore the complexity of reality, and unearth the underlying structures of privilege and suppression that have been central to the experience of people of color in U.S. society.

Pause to Reflect

What messages about race, racism, systems of power, oppression, and justice do you bring into your classroom? Whose voices are privileged, and whose are missing? What narratives do you teach, and what stories do you challenge? What media documents about race and racism do you have your students decode, and why? What will you include, and what will you (inevitably) leave out in constructing your implicitly and explicitly mediated curriculum of race?

The exploration of race in America must include a deep look at Whiteness, lest the central characters and motivations behind systemic racism remain invisible. We need to involve students in appropriate ways of understanding the role that White privilege and White people have played in constructing systems of lies, distortions, and stereotypes about race. We need students to understand the economics of race and how it has motivated systems of thinking and policy. And we need to have students analyze messages about those who have resisted these systems: African American leaders and everyday Black heroes; Indigenous peoples of the past and present; patriotic Latinx people, Asian Americans, and members of other ethnic groups who have demanded equality; as well as courageous White people who have committed their lives to the struggle for racial justice. When Whiteness is singularly represented through supporters of White supremacy, White students are more likely to be mired in shame and guilt.

The challenge of balancing all these varied messages can be overwhelming, as is the fullness of U.S. history. Ultimately, we can only do our best to bring appropriate, diverse, and thoughtful media choices into our classrooms that will push students in the complexity of their thinking, in their empathy and compassion, and in their motivation to make the world a more just and loving place.

As the research of Kahne and Bowyer (2017), described in Chapter 1, has shown, motivated reasoning (including confirmation bias) interferes with students' abilities to accurately evaluate political claims. Similarly, our students' views of race will not necessarily be swayed by showing them our mediated truths. They need to also reflect on their own interpretations and biases, and how their life experience and identities have affected their views. In the words of one high school student speaking about media decoding, "It's helped me learn because I can hear other people's opinions and maybe I can make connections with it [and] agree or disagree, so it helps me have more of an open mind." This openness to rethinking one's views can be facilitated through skillful leading of media decoding activities that tap into critical issues, such as systemic racism. They can be provoked when students develop the habits of asking "What makes me say that?" "How do my peers think differently, and why?" "What are the influences on my interpretations, and what are my biases?" "How do I justify my views?" When these questions are applied to media decoding of messages about race and racism, our students are more likely to evolve in their thinking.

Lessons for Change

The CMD process gives teachers both the methodology and the classroom materials to bring complex pictures of racial oppression and enfranchisement into the classroom. Teachers can use engaging media documents, relevant to the developmental levels and identities of their students and their subject-area content, to teach complex understandings about the systemic nature of racism, the history of oppression, exemplars of resistance, and models for change.

Figure 7.3 gives examples of CMD activities available on the Project Look Sharp website that address the complex and challenging issues of race and racism. Although many of the lessons on this list center on the African American experience, we include lessons about Native Americans and Latinx, White, and other people that address issues of race and racism. Our intent is to show the types of media documents, topics, and themes that can be addressed in different subject areas and at different grade levels. We hope that educators will use these models to help create their own media decoding activities.

The last lesson, *Media Representations of Working-Class Men,* deserves some explanation. Although it names social class as the primary focus, it is fundamentally about *White* working-class men and the changing popular cultural representations of them over time. It examines representations that have helped fuel the resentments of many White working men (and women) who feel victimized by the "liberal urban elite." Because this lesson, like others in the list, would likely raise issues that electrify the nation's current political polarization, you will need to judge the readiness of your class for this work. Are they ready to enter into this decoding in

---

FIGURE 7.3 Project Look Sharp's CMD Lessons About Racism

Elementary Level

Phillis Wheatley's Poem. Students analyze a poem, written in 1773 by America's first published African American poet, comparing the American revolution with the struggle against slavery.

(https://projectlooksharp.org/wheatley)

Squanto and the First Thanksgiving: Whose Story? Students analyze excerpts from children's books for differing perspectives and messages about the history of Thanksgiving.

(https://projectlooksharp.org/squanto)

Unearthing Stereotypes. Using a handout and slides, students identify whether each of 12 photos is from Africa or not and then reflect on the sources of stereotypical thinking.

(https://projectlooksharp.org/Africaphotos)

Middle School and High School Level

Environmental Justice—For Whom, How, and Why? In this science and humanities lesson, students analyze video messages about impacts of and potential remedies for environmental justice.

(https://projectlooksharp.org/envjustice)

Huracán María. In this Spanish-language lesson, students analyze excerpts of newspaper articles about Puerto Rican climate refugees in Florida.

(https://projectlooksharp.org/huracanmaria)

Questioning Manifest Destiny. Students analyze diverse media imagery about efforts to oppose manifest destiny during the Indian Wars, the Mexican War, and the Philippine–American War.

(https://projectlooksharp.org/manifest)

Mapping the Border: Who Decides? Students analyze different maps of the U.S.- Mexico border region for indicators about how mapmakers use images and words to convey messages.

(https://projectlooksharp.org/mapborder)

Unions and Race. In this economics and history lesson, students analyze four short film excerpts about racial inclusion and exclusion in the labor union movement between 1910 and 1920.

(https://projectlooksharp.org/unionsrace)

Carry Me to Freedom. Students analyze four short song excerpts for messages about the movement to abolish slavery in the United States in the early and mid-19th century.
(https://projectlooksharp.org/carryfreedom)

Decoding the Twenty: Andrew Jackson and Harriet Tubman. Students analyze images related to the 20-dollar bill for messages about U.S. history and historical context.
(https://projectlooksharp.org/twenty)

Thanksgiving: Who's Telling the Story? Students analyze short videos for messages about the meanings and impacts of the stories surrounding Thanksgiving.
(https://projectlooksharp.org/thanksgiving)

High School and College Level

Representations of Enslavement in South Carolina. Students analyze primary and secondary texts from the 19th, 20th, and 21st centuries for messages about African slavery.
(https://projectlooksharp.org/southcarolina)

Sustainable Cultures. Students analyze websites and videos about sustainable agricultural practices among traditional land-based cultures.
(https://projectlooksharp.org/sustaincultures)

Disease Spreads: Cholera Epidemic of 1892. In this health, science, journalism, and history lesson, students analyze an 1890 anti-Semitic cartoon and editorial and excerpts from a current magazine article and medical webpage to examine beliefs about the spread of disease.
(https://projectlooksharp.org/cholera)

Creativity in Preserving Cultural Tradition. Students analyze four short film excerpts about the roles of elders in preserving cultural traditions.
(https://projectlooksharp.org/tradition)

Confrontation in the Streets: What Do You Know? Students analyze their own biases after examining a viral social media video and a TV news program on the same event.
(https://projectlooksharp.org/confrontation)

Media Representations of Working-Class Men. Students analyze a 1930s mural and a 1990s clip from *The Simpsons* TV show for messages about working-class men.
(https://projectlooksharp.org/workingclass)

Source: © 2019 Project Look Sharp. Used with permission.

a way that will lead to dialogue that is, in the words of Paulo Freire, "loving, humble, hopeful, trusting, and critical" rather than "loveless, arrogant, hopeless, mistrustful, acritical" (Freire & Macedo, 1998, p. 84)? The same is true about many of the other Project Look Sharp lessons that tap into codes of oppression and resilience related to gender, sexual orientation, ability, religion, geography, national origin, immigration, and the many other reflections of our complex identities.

Although the risks are real for teaching about these challenging topics in a way that promotes honest emotions and perspectives, the risks of not doing so are evident in the profound divisions that consistently wrack the nation. As a critical foundation of U.S. democracy, schools must rise to the occasion to help educate a generation that is able to express higher levels of civility, justice, and truth.

VOICES FOR CHANGE: SUPPORTING CMD IN YOUR SCHOOL AND DISTRICT

It is one thing to integrate constructivist media decoding into our own teaching practice but another entirely to attempt to integrate it into the practice of a department, grade-level team, school, or district. The premise of this book is that we need to have the habits of critical thinking about all media messages integrated across and throughout the curriculum.

With that goal in mind, this closing chapter explores how to incorporate constructivist media decoding throughout a school or district. We look at the role of teacher leaders—including librarians—as advocates of media literacy integration, and we explore professional development strategies for promoting CMD throughout the curriculum. In the final section, we highlight the voices of educators and students as they reflect on the impact of this work on teaching and learning, and we end by looking at the role of media literacy in democratic citizenship and empowerment. If you feel passionate about the imperative of developing media literacy in every student, consider taking a leadership role in your school or district to help bring it about.

Leadership and School Change

If you are a teacher, a librarian, a curriculum chair, an instructional coach, an administrator, or another school leader, you can play a key role in infusing media analysis across the curriculum. As with any school change, your work will take time, involving listening and responding to the needs of key stakeholders and working backward from your goals to develop and implement strategies for successful long-term change. Among the questions to ask in conceptualizing media literacy integration throughout a school or district are the following:

- What are your short-term and long-term goals?
- Who and what will you target? Will you collaborate with a few staff, seed a few exemplars, work with a specific grade-level team or subject-area department, pursue curricular integration, attempt to influence leadership, seek whole-school change, provide district or regional professional development, persuade a regional or subject-area organization to support your effort?
- How can you most successfully work with them? Can you use team meetings (curriculum, department, grade level), one-on-one sessions, staff meetings, directives from above, getting on an agenda?
- What professional development opportunities do you have to work with staff? Can you use inter-staff communication, presentations at meetings (whole staff, grade level, subject area), district or regional professional development, a multisession course?
- Who needs to be on board, and who are your potential allies? Can you get support from the principal, other administrators, the librarian, department chairs, team leaders, parents, the school board, regional professional development folks, organizations?
- Are there upcoming curricular changes or professional development initiatives that can help facilitate media literacy integration? Is there a new curriculum, a district project, work related to new standards, a new state mandate, work related to assessment?

- What opportunities do you anticipate? Where will you get support? What resources can you tap? What motivations can you leverage?
- What challenges do you anticipate? Where will you likely face resistance? What concerns will be raised? How might you respond?
- What resources and support do you need? What are your needs personally, economically, and organizationally? What time is needed by whom? What media literacy support do you need from whom?

Opportunities for Integration

Just as we must listen well to the meaning making of our students, we must listen well to how our target groups think about media literacy integration, including those with the power to support or undermine our goals and those who are most critical to making it happen. What are their priorities and motivations, and what language will help to bring them on board as allies and collaborators? Although it will be helpful if they are motivated by the imperatives of media literacy, that is not necessarily a prerequisite.

Schools are overwhelmed with multiple and often competing priorities. Where the leadership in a school or district can be swayed to prioritize media literacy integration, we have a lot of arguments we can use. The sheer volume of teen media use today is shocking—even to those of us in media literacy education. Before the global pandemic and school shutdowns, the average U.S. teenager consumed nearly 10 hours a day of media, not including media use during school or for homework (Common Sense Media, 2019). We know that media use has skyrocketed for all age groups during the pandemic (World Economic Forum, 2020). New technologies such as smartphones give children access to media nearly 24/7, challenging their nervous systems to cope with incessant pinging for attention. The algorithms that drive our media diet push a consumption of potentially harmful and often inaccurate messages. CMD provides strategies that will address these concerns in the context of schools' mounting crush of responsibilities. But it is likely we will need to have an additional rationale for integrating media literacy into the curriculum, and it should tap into the needs of a diverse constituency.

Curriculum Standards

Every state has its curriculum standards, codified language for what we should be prioritizing in our teaching. We also have national standards for different disciplines, crafted or supported by teaching organizations, such as the NCSS *College, Career, and Civic Life (C3) Framework for Social Studies State Standards* (2021), or the NSTA *Next Generation Science Standards* (2021). The *Common Core State Standards* (2021) outline national standards for English and mathematics. All of these include a growing emphasis on teaching critical thinking, providing an opening for the integration of media literacy into curriculum and instruction.

As we noted in Chapter 2, media literacy skills can be identified in all the contemporary disciplinary standards of the major national organizations and, we suspect, in the teaching and learning standards for all 50 states. Media analysis skills have a place in the standards when we see the terms *analysis* and *evaluation,* as well as *inquiry, questioning,* and *curiosity.* These standards can be a defense of—and an argument for—the integration of media analysis into the curriculum.

The teaching of critical thinking is not an add-on to the curriculum but a core expectation in 21st century education. CMD can provide a specific, accessible, and proven methodology for teaching standards-driven critical-thinking skills in diverse subjects and grade levels. District or statewide work on new standards can offer an opening for media literacy integration, particularly if it is accompanied by curricular changes.

Pause to Reflect

What kind of leadership and support would your school need in order to integrate CMD and other aspects of media literacy across the curriculum? How might you take a leadership role in that process?

New Curriculum Materials

One of the prime opportunities to incorporate media analysis into the curriculum is when schools or districts put resources into developing new curriculum materials. The following examples illustrate how different curriculum-related catalysts led to the integration of media literacy into the humanities curriculum of a relatively small upstate New York school district. In all of these examples, teachers, librarians, schools, district administrators, and organizations needed to create new materials to address curricular changes and needs. They were delighted to have the integration of critical thinking about diverse and engaging media documents be an accompanying goal of the work, but none of them had media literacy as their primary motivation. Here are the examples:

- First grade teachers needed new materials that reflected the growing diversity of the families in the district. This resulted in the family curriculum described in Chapter 7.
- Third grade teachers needed new curriculum materials to address the new state standards for teaching about Africa. This resulted in the 3rd grade Africa lessons referenced in Chapter 4.
- A district interdisciplinary "case study" initiative enabled a media literacy question (*How do we know what we know?*) to be the uniting theme for a 6th grade schoolwide unit on Rome, described in Chapter 7.
- A district's need to address conflicting ideological views on the teaching of economics resulted in critical-thinking/media literacy lessons that integrate the CMD approach into the 8th grade U.S. history curriculum (see the Project Look Sharp kit *Economics in U.S. History*, at https://projectlooksharp.org/economics).
- The need for educational resources related to a "community read" of a book by Martin Luther King Jr. resulted in a team of educators crafting a lesson that prepared 11th graders for the New York State ELA Regents Exam through decoding three speeches by King (see

the lesson *Three Speeches,* in the kit *Media Constructions of Martin Luther King Jr.,* at https://projectlooksharp.org/mlk3speeches).

Although these examples mostly focus on social studies and English, there are likely to be similar opportunities for integration into science, health, global languages, arts, and a host of other subject areas. As advocates of media literacy, we should always be looking for opportunities for curriculum-driven integration that will raise a media-literate, curious, reflective, metacognitive, and empowered generation of young people. But this work will require the creativity, knowledge, and commitment of media literacy advocates within our schools and districts.

Librarians as Leaders for Media Literacy

Media literacy should be integrated in all subject areas and grade levels. Media analysis should be taught everywhere—but because of that, it risks being taught nowhere. For media and information literacy to be integrated everywhere, it needs a champion, a curricular and instructional leader. Such leaders can be most effective when they have connections to all students and teachers throughout the building, when they are involved in teaching and curriculum development, when they are skilled at research and finding resources, and when they understand the discipline of media literacy. Librarians are the logical leaders of media literacy in their schools. Here are two stories that illustrate the wisdom of having librarians as media literacy advocates.

In the late 1990s, Project Look Sharp began a multiyear project in collaboration with the Onondaga Nation and the Ithaca City School District to create materials for a 4th grade unit on the Iroquois, the Haudenosaunee people of upstate New York. The kit was to include lessons about respect and the stereotyping of Native Peoples in the media. Chris mentioned the project to June Locke, the librarian at his daughter's elementary school. June excused herself for a moment and went to get some books in the back of a closet. In collaboration with her teachers, she had periodically removed books from the library shelves, including those with derogatory messages about Native Americans. June had not discarded the books but held on to them, foreseeing just this possibility. Those books became the anchor documents for our media literacy lesson on cultural respect and disrespect, still used to this day in Ithaca. As a librarian, she had a keen sense of the utility of historical representations in teaching students to decode biases in children's literature.

In the early 2000s, Chris invited Margaret Hohenstein, the librarian at his school, to be one of the raters for the final performance of his 10th grade humanities class. All students at the Lehman Alternative Community School in Ithaca are deemed ready for graduation through portfolios and performances of skill and knowledge rather than credits. After sitting through a few presentations, Margaret told Chris that he really should hold every student accountable for knowing the source of every fact they present, as well as the credibility of each source. Chris thought that undertaking was too difficult (in part because he was not able to do that in his own presentations), but he was intrigued. Over the next few years, Chris instituted that requirement for the presentations, and sure enough, the 10th graders rose to the challenge. Today, LACS high school students come prepared to explain, at any point during their performance, where their information and analysis come from and how they know that the sources are credible.

Both June and Margaret were successful advocates for media and information literacy. They taught the "media literacy expert" (Chris) how the job needed to be done. More than anyone else in the building, librarians are positioned to be the advocates, researchers, supporters, coaches, and trainers for media literacy integration. Media and information literacy is their discipline. Yes, librarians have many other responsibilities. They have become the stewards of technology integration at our schools, monitoring issues of digital access and privacy and often taking on the burdens of tech support in under-resourced buildings. They oversee the space we call the library, stewarding our shared collection of books and other media. They have budgetary responsibilities and often act as key liaisons with the community outside the school. They are building-based educational leaders for curriculum, instruction, and assessment. And those are just their formal roles.

So how can we expect librarians to step into the role of media literacy advocates, coaches, and trainers for our schools? We can do so because no one else in the building is capable of doing the job: working across all grades and subjects; networking with teachers, support staff, and administration; leveraging changes in curriculum; understanding the nuances of school culture, personalities, and structures for change. Although it is no small lift, librarians should take on the role of media literacy leader in their building if for no other reason than that it makes the role of the librarian undeniably essential to the aims of an equitable, just, and liberal education.

The 2020 report by Democracy Ready NY, *Developing Digital Citizens: Media Literacy Education for All Students,* puts the full and equitable funding of librarians in all New York schools at the center of its advocacy for media literacy. The report recommends that "all schools be staffed with a library media specialist who can provide media literacy instruction for students at each grade level, as well as training for teachers across the curriculum" (p. 23), that "school library media specialists should be expected to teach media literacy and support classroom teachers in teaching media literacy" (p. 12), and that they "should receive specific training in how to work with all teachers in their schools to integrate media literacy effectively into curriculum and instruction" (p. 34). But how can our librarians, or other curriculum leaders in our schools, take leadership in integrating media literacy equitably and sustainably across the curriculum?

Professional Development for Media Literacy Integration

In the early 2000s, we at Project Look Sharp hoped that the publication of high-quality, user-friendly, easily searchable, free lessons would facilitate the effective integration of media literacy. For many teachers, this has been true. But outside evaluations of the use of our materials and our own experience with teachers have shown that most educators need some training to effectively and appropriately incorporate question-based media analysis into their teaching. The gravitational pull of the traditional "banking" methods of teaching that most of us grew up with is strong, as are the tendencies to use media to illustrate and entertain rather than as a source of analysis. Leading a truly constructivist, student-centered collective analysis with objectives-based probing for evidence typically requires training, practice, coaching, practice, reflecting, and more practice. Like any authentic shift in teaching, it requires time and resources. But the time and resources needed can be integrated with existing structures and initiatives such as project-based learning, differentiation, performance-based assessment, online learning, and cultural competency.

Grade-level teams and subject-area departments are good places to start when growing media literacy in a school. At the elementary level, most schools have regular grade-level team meetings where targeted professional development can be delivered. Having the support of the team and the team leader will be critical in getting time on the agenda. Similarly, for subject-area or department meetings, typically at the secondary level, the first step is to get some time dedicated to professional development for media literacy integration. As we have already stated, it may be new curricular mandates, standards, instructional initiatives, or assessments that provide an opening for training your staff in CMD theory and practice. Any exposure to the benefits of media literacy integration can open the door for continued work, but the best PD approaches involve sustained experience with classroom practice and reflection.

Although inspirational one-time presentations can provoke pedagogical growth for some teachers, we know that the impact of professional development increases with sustained work that is implemented in the classroom with repeated reflection, revision, and practice. This observation has certainly been Project Look Sharp's experience with successful professional development. When possible, advocates should plan media literacy PD that includes initial training and modeling, followed by collaborative teacher-generated curriculum design, followed by classroom implementation. This PD should include reflection, ideally in small groups, to identify and celebrate successes and problem-solve challenges. Throughout the process, a media literacy coach can keep the PD moving forward by helping teachers to establish realistic goals, make and revise plans and benchmarks, and codify their learning. It is an added benefit when a coach can support the work by researching useful media documents or lessons for upcoming units. It was just this type of collaboration that led to the *Spider-Man vs. Hydro-Man* lesson highlighted at the beginning of Chapter 1.

Public performance of learning, such as a presentation to colleagues or the publication of a lesson, can be a motivating component of professional development. The expectation of producing a final product to be shared can be a key factor in keeping educators motivated to meet regularly and continue an initiative despite daily pressures and priorities. The scheduling of short but periodic meetings with a coach, virtually or in person, also helps to keep educators on track and gives them ideas, resources, and an opportunity for reflection when they get stuck. Online platforms such as Zoom can be a terrific resource for regular coaching, and as we have learned during the pandemic shutdowns, face-to-face relationships carry their own power.

Media Decoding with Colleagues

The best demonstration of the effectiveness of constructivist media decoding during professional development is to have colleagues experience the process themselves, as students. Opening a PD session with an engaging media decoding activity is arguably the best way to ensure engagement and buy-in for the rest of the training while modeling the CMD process. If time is limited, this activity can be brief.

When we work with high school social studies teachers, we often start by leading a decoding of the opening credits to Disney's 1992 movie *Aladdin* with this prompt: "What are the messages in this clip about the Arab world, and what is your evidence?" We typically show just the first 15 seconds of the opening credits: Arabic music playing over red and orange flames behind the title *Aladdin* in a stylized font that disappears in a whirl of smoke. Despite seeing only a few seconds of the "text," the participants quickly volunteer messages about the *alien, exotic,* perhaps *sensual* or *dangerous foreign place* conjured up by the images and sounds. Meanwhile, the facilitator follows up those responses with evidence-based questions: "What makes you say that?" "Where did you see that in the document?" For some responses—for instance, "It shows the Arab world as foreign"— the facilitator might prompt, "If you agree, raise your hand" and then engage otherwise quiet colleagues in participating in the decoding.

This activity can take less than five minutes, but it illustrates the role of a skillful facilitator in addressing many qualities of good teaching, including student engagement, effective questioning, listening to student meaning making, document-based analysis, and diversifying texts. It is important to take some time to debrief at least one of the early decoding activities in your PD session: "Why was this so engaging?" "Would our students get into this?" "How could this activity teach key social studies concepts and knowledge (e.g., stereotyping in the media)?" "How can we use this approach to teach to other standards and content?" "Can we take the time from our curriculum to do this kind of thing?" The five-minute decoding activity will prompt the participants to engage with these important questions.

One of the best strategies we have found for effective training in leading media decoding activities is to have teachers develop their own CMD plan for a 7- to 10-minute activity and practice leading it, with their colleagues acting as students. The crafting of a CMD activity plan, as described in Chapter 3, asks the teacher to think ahead about potential student responses and follow-up probes. Doing so prepares a teacher to lead an objectives-directed, question-based, evidence-driven collective analysis of media documents. Practicing a short activity, with other educators acting as students, highlights the challenges of real decoding in a supportive and educational environment. The follow-up 10- to 15-minute debriefing of the decoding, beginning with the facilitator's self-reflections, can make transparent subtle and important aspects of the teaching process. The debriefing is not meant to be evaluative, and it is important to support each facilitator; but "cool" (critical or questioning) as well as "warm" (affirming) feedback will likely deepen the learning for all involved. Ideally, all members of a training will have the opportunity to lead a practice decoding, but the process of participating in the decoding and the debriefing can be a deep learning experience for all participants, not just the "teacher."

Time, Documents, and Resources for PD

The CMD process responds directly to the perennial teacher concern that "we just don't have the time." Our tendency as teachers is to want to be more interactive and engaging, but we often let go of that aim when we feel the inevitable pressure to "cover the curriculum."

We get this response most often at the high school level from the teachers of content-heavy subjects such as science and social studies. A well-done demonstration of media decoding can effectively address this concern head-on. When working with social studies teachers, we often show a short, annotated video demonstrating 10th grade students decoding two maps—one from a Palestinian website and one from an Israeli website. In less than five minutes, the students collectively discover that maps can have a bias in the facts they choose to present and how those facts are presented. Few social studies teachers would suggest that one could teach this important concept as effectively—and in less time—using another methodology. On the Project Look Sharp website, you will find more than a dozen short, annotated *Demonstration Videos* like this that illustrate the leading of CMD activities at different grade levels and for different subject areas. These can be useful in PD trainings.

The choice of what media documents to decode during a PD training is an important one. The more targeted the group (e.g., all 2nd grade teachers or all high school ELA teachers), the easier it is to ensure that all of the practice decodings are relevant to all the participants. Although it is most helpful for participants to see examples that relate to the grade level and content they are teaching, if the audience of educators is heterogeneous, use decoding activities that model key aspects of CMD and that can apply to all participants.

You should also consider whether or not to share media decoding examples that touch on challenging topics. Media decoding can be a particularly effective approach for dealing with potentially divisive issues such as racism, politics, climate change, and body image. In working with teachers who struggle with how to maintain civil discourse or address confirmation biases with their students, demonstrating the boundaries and academic protocols of CMD can be a hook. But demonstrating media decodings of these issues can leave the impression that CMD is exclusively for teaching older students about tough issues. It is important to understand that it can be used as effectively to teach nearly any content at any age, including non-controversial topics such as the qualities of liquid matter, even at 1st grade.

When designing a media literacy PD experience, we will not always have the opportunity to build in the time for collaboration, theory, creativity, practice, reflection, and performance. Some PD work can be designed merely to inspire teachers to consider taking on a project, or to present them with resources they can access on their own. Other short PD experiences can include having colleagues collaborate to identify decoding questions related to a specific media document; reflect on how they already incorporate metacognition about media messages into their curriculum; or decode a rich media document related to issues the school is grappling with. Although we should seek all opportunities for long-term, sustainable, and fully resourced professional development, keeping media literacy on the agenda and in the consciousness of our colleagues may require lots of short, repeated, and fun experiences that teach them about the benefits of integrating media decoding into our classrooms.

There are a number of excellent online resources for compelling media literacy activities and professional development. The website for Media Literacy Now (2021) includes an annotated listing of media literacy organizations and resources for educators and librarians, as well as resources for parents. The National Association for Media Literacy Education (2021) is another excellent gateway to media literacy organizations and advocacy. Many media literacy organizations have excellent resources for media production as well as analysis, but Project Look Sharp is the only source for the CMD approach that is the focus of this book. Among the free resources available at www.projectlooksharp.org are the following:

- More than 500 media literacy lessons searchable by keyword, subject, grade level, standard, media type, and so on. You can share groups of lessons with your teachers (e.g., all lessons for high school science on climate change, or all lessons on nutrition for the primary grades) by completing a search for the targeted lessons on the Project Look Sharp site, copying the URL for the search, and forwarding it to your teachers.
- Short, annotated videos demonstrating the leading of media decoding activities for different grade levels and subject areas (see *Demonstration Videos* on the Project Look Sharp homepage).
- Handouts, including *Key Questions to Ask When Analyzing Media Messages* and *Key Questions to Ask When Creating Media Messages* (PDFs for posters are also available); *6 Key Concepts in Media Analysis; Media Literacy Objectives; Tips for Decoding;* and more.
- Articles and webinars about constructivist media decoding and a DIY (Do It Yourself) Guide for creating your own CMD lessons.

In addition, the *Constructivist Media Decoding Guide* (shown in Figure 8.1, pp. 164–165) identifies specific rules, considerations, tips, and cautions for media decoding that should assist anyone working with teachers and colleagues in designing and delivering media decoding activities.

Shifting Teaching Practice

The integration of CMD can help to shift teaching practice in many different ways. For example, it

- Provides a defined protocol for focusing on questioning rather than telling, having students be the workers in the job of critical analysis.

- Has educators practice objectives-driven teaching, working backward from their goals to design and deliver lessons that target specific standards.
- Integrates literacy with content through interdisciplinary learning that can fit easily in subject-specific classes.
- Teaches evidence-based analysis of diverse documents.
- Trains educators to use many different modes of instruction to target the diverse learning styles and needs of their students.
- Teaches teachers to elicit information from their students about how they understand and how they learn.
- Enables teachers to teach students to be metacognitive about their own thinking.
- Guides teachers in their shift to an inquiry-based pedagogy.

CMD is flexible in its use and easily adaptable to many different contexts and needs. Media decoding activities can be used for different purposes: as a hook when introducing a new unit, as periodic enrichment activities, for teaching core subject-area skills and content, and for assessment. Given the current polarization of cultural identities in U.S. society, CMD can be an effective strategy for addressing challenging topics in the classroom, building skills in fact-based analysis while listening to the views of others. Training teachers in the pedagogy and process of constructivist media decoding can be a "thin slice" approach to educational change. If our colleagues can become comfortable with this inquiry-based, constructivist approach to media analysis, that outcome can help to promote larger pedagogical shifts within a school. Whether advocating for the integration of CMD into new curriculum, for its use as a methodology within another initiative, for tackling challenging topics, for deepening classroom engagement for *all* students, or for the sole purpose of teaching habits of media literacy and critical thinking, it will be important to have a good understanding of the effects that this approach has on teachers and students.

FIGURE 8.1 Constructivist Media Decoding Guide

Rules
- **Start with your objectives** for the activity. Define a small number of subject-area and media literacy objectives. Choose your media document(s), formulate your questions, and write a decoding plan aligned with these objectives.
- **Keep it constructivist** by focusing on questions. Have students do the analysis, apply knowledge, and discover key concepts collectively.

Considerations in Choosing Media Documents
- Do they address your subject-area and media literacy objectives?
- Do they offer rich opportunities for student analysis and engagement?
- Are they of sufficient quality/clarity to allow students to read the information you are asking about?
- What background knowledge will students need to do the decoding you intend?
- Have you vetted the documents for accuracy and sourcing?
- Are they appropriate for your students? Have you considered the potential for reinforcing negative messages, misinterpretation, or triggering of painful memories?

Use Media Decoding for Different Purposes, such as...
- Providing an engaging hook for a new unit.
- Unearthing prior knowledge or perceptions.
- Teaching new knowledge or concepts.
- Preparing students for producing media.
- Assessing student learning.

Decide Your Approach to Decoding, such as...
- Individual decoding in writing (in class or as a homework assignment).
- Paired or small-group work.
- Individual or small-group analysis to prepare for leading a whole-group decoding.
- Whole-group decoding.
- Reviewing the document more than once, with discussion after each viewing/reading.

Develop Questions That...
- Address your objectives.
- Ask students to apply content knowledge.
- Elicit evidence from the document.
- Are varied in complexity and scaffolded to engage all students.
- Emphasize higher-order skills by being open to varied interpretations.
- Target growth in student thinking.
- Promote metacognition.

Develop a Decoding Plan That...
- Is aligned with your content objectives (e.g., *What are the messages about _____?*).
- Is aligned with your literacy objectives [see Figure 4.1, p. 59].

- Includes probing for evidence where applicable (e.g., *What makes you say that?*).
- Anticipates potential student responses.
- Anticipates potential for emotional responses or hurtful comments.
- Considers strategies for involving all students.
- Considers strategies for having students talk directly to each other, asking their own questions and challenging each other's thinking.

Consider These Cautions

- Don't tell students what to see; ask questions instead.
- Don't set them up to feel stupid.

- Help them to analyze free from your judgments.
- Listen for resistance (e.g., when a student says, "You are reading into this").
- Contrast negative or potentially harmful messages with positive messages (decode both).
- "Do no harm." Be aware of the power of media messages and the potential for unintended consequences (e.g., reinforcing stereotypes or decoding potentially harmful messages).
- Cue into and follow up with students' emotional responses to documents.
- Listen carefully to the meaning making of your students.

Source: © 2019 Project Look Sharp. Used with permission.

The Impacts of CMD— What Students and Teachers Say

The best evidence of the impacts of ongoing CMD integration in the classroom have come from comments by teachers and students themselves. The following quotes come from their reflections on the impact of the process of constructivist media decoding.

Teachers often comment on how CMD enfranchises a broad range of students, but especially those alienated by traditional classroom methodologies. In evaluating a yearlong initiative that trained science teachers and librarians to integrate media literacy, participants shared the following observations:

- "Every level of student wanted to respond."
- "This was able to reach kids who were more 'English/language arts type' students than just the typical 'science type' students."

- "Some of the students who struggled most with literacy skills and feeling comfortable participating in the classroom deeply engaged with this lesson. The whole class, but those kids especially, blew us away with their depth of thought and ability to analyze the media."

The CMD approach enables students with diverse learning styles to challenge negative self-perceptions that can be fostered by heavily print-dependent methodologies and standardized testing. One of Chris's high school students regularly talked about himself as "being dumb." He scored poorly on most traditional tests but was highly engaged in the media decoding process. In the spring when the class was analyzing current news photos, he commented, "This is just like how Secretary of Defense McNamara was presented in the 1965 photo from the Vietnam War." He went on to describe the similarities between the two photos and compared their contexts. We had spent only a few minutes decoding that McNamara image—six months earlier. So much for "being dumb."

The use of diverse media for classroom analysis can empower students to become more active learners. As one high school student commented: "I never knew how curious of a person I was in my own learning or how interested I was in things I never thought I would be interested in until I started looking at it through different mediums."

Both teachers and students regularly comment on the role of the CMD process in teaching independent thinking. The following comments come from high school students who have had extensive experience in inquiry-based media analysis:

- "Media literacy teaching is different in that it's more interactive, it's more the students doing their own personal thinking as opposed to having a teacher writing it up on a board—this is the answer."
- "It doesn't feel like the teacher is just giving you the information; it feels like they are helping you to figure it out for yourself."
- "Instead of just having a teacher tell the students what something is supposed to mean and how it is supposed to be, it allows the students

to question that and to think for themselves and really have their own ideas."

- "In every school, teachers are going to have their own biases, and I think that it's really important for students to be able to create their own opinions."

The decoding experience can hone students' academic abilities, including skills not overtly related to media analysis, as illustrated in the following quotes:

- "When I'm doing research projects now, I'm going to look at the biases first, and because most of the time students just go straight to the internet and the first thing that pops up in your Google search is the one that you use, but now I think that I'm going to have to really analyze it and understand the bias and then get another point of view and then base my opinions off the two different points of view."
- "It also helps you break apart that information and be more critical about it and construct your own thesis because you've been doing it with media literacy in high school, and then when you go on and you're expected to write a thesis paper, you will already know how to break apart information and how to form your own opinions on it and you know how to look at all sides and you know what you think is right and wrong."

Often, students comment on the relevance of media literacy to their lives outside school. These comments are not always positive, as illustrated by the time a student accused Chris of ruining their enjoyment of movies because they couldn't stop thinking about the intent of the filmmakers and how each shot was constructed: "I would go to the mall and notice every detail." But most of the time, students appreciated the influence of media decoding on their lives, as these comments illustrate:

- "I think being able to analyze how much power media has over what we learn, knowing how it works, is so important to understanding how we live life."

- "Media literacy teaches our generation, really any generation, about how to interact in this new society we are building."

Perhaps the most consistent comments about the impact of media decoding from high school students had to do with learning to think critically about the world. Here are some examples:

- "I'm more aware, I'm looking for everything behind the media, not just what it is actually saying."
- "We had to look at everything from multiple perspectives and pay close attention to the reason behind things."
- "It has given me a lot more tools to critically examine what I see in the world, what I see in advertisements, what I see in my own actions."
- "At other schools, it's more like, here's a textbook, this is true, and at our school, we really learn how to even question what we're being taught."
- "I no longer view the world from a single standpoint, and I am able to identify and empathize with multiple perspectives. I can comprehend why individuals have certain biases, and all the while question my own."

One concern that comes up regularly for educators when learning about media literacy is the potential for promoting cynicism by teaching students to habitually question all media messages. Although our intent is to promote skepticism, not cynicism, this concern is real. Our intent should not be to teach students to continually distrust authority, to embrace relativism, or to reject all impassioned speech. Open-mindedness should not be confused with nihilism. But we must listen to students' authentic and challenging questions and address them with caution and honesty. We risk unintentionally fueling cynicism in students, particularly teenagers, when we avoid addressing the issues that dominate their adolescent epistemological curriculum.

The following story speaks to the risks but also the benefits of teaching teenagers to question their worlds. During the final reflections at the end of Chris's yearlong 10th grade media literacy and humanities class, one student spoke about her loss of innocence. She explained that she had begun the year thinking that she could change everything broken in the world, but that the class had "shattered her rose-colored glasses." Chris remembers being momentarily devastated by her comment. But when she saw the look on his face, the young woman added, "But it's OK. They needed to be broken." She explained that although the learning was painful and she missed her unbridled optimism, she was grateful to understand the complexities and to see the world more clearly.

The whole time this student was speaking, the girl next to her, a quite unfiltered and edgy teenager with many piercings and tattoos, was struggling not to interrupt. When Chris finally called on her, she explained, "It is so interesting what she said, because for me I entered the class thinking that everything is totally f----d up, the media is all manipulated, and that there was no real right or wrong. I still think that everything is f----d up, but this class taught me that some things are more manipulated than others and that some things are more wrong than others."

Although we cannot protect our students, particularly our adolescents, from the true nature of the world, we can work to facilitate a supportive and respectful classroom ecology in which they have the opportunity to grow into their adult skins. The CMD process fosters authentic dialogue among peers about issues of real concern, and that dialogue can build a foundation for collective growth.

Perhaps the greatest impact that media decoding can have on students is on their sense of themselves as lifelong learners. Consider these comments:

- "Media literacy is different from other forms of teaching because it's literally like teaching you how to learn."
- "It just changes the way I look at things, everything... it changes the way my eyes work, pretty much, it teaches me how to learn in a sense

because it's teaching me how to watch and how to look, keep a mindful eye and how to be aware."

- "You see something in a published magazine, and you assume, oh, this must be the truth.... But in the school we go to, I've learned to question that, and to say things like... why, ya know, just ask the question... *why.*"

The Imperatives for Teaching Students to Decode Their World

We hope that the voices and the stories in this book will inspire educators to embrace the potential of media decoding to empower individual students. By diversifying our texts, by compelling our students to inquire about the purpose, meaning, and impact of social messages, we have students practice the habits of thinking that can lead to more informed, more complex, and more thoughtful action. Although we as educators prioritize the growth, self-esteem, and capacity of each of our students, the effort must be in the context of the broader society. Personal empowerment should ultimately benefit everyone.

At the heart of our democratic promise of individual and collective empowerment is a mutual commitment to universal education. The founders of the United States understood the centrality of literacy to citizenship in a democracy. They understood that the ability to decode social messages was a prerequisite for the growth of informed civic agency. There is no clearer reflection of their understanding of this link than the denial of literacy, education, and citizenship to African Americans in service of the entrenched economic and political interests of slavery. To reach the full promise of our democracy, we must pursue the full meaning of literacy in contemporary culture.

Today's literacy, education, and democratic citizenship are all dependent upon teaching students to read their fast-changing world. We have moved beyond the newspaper as the primary mode of mass-mediated information, beyond radio, beyond TV. At some point, we will move beyond the internet and social media—at least as we know them today. But we will not move beyond literacy or education or citizenship. Whatever form mass media takes in shaping future generations, individuals will need the skills, habits, and motivation to ask hard and compelling questions about meaning making, power, and their own learning.

In a sense, media literacy is as old as humanity. When women and men painted representations of their world in caves 30,000 years ago, when they crafted complex stories about the origins of humanity, when they passed forward words on a printed page, they were creating mediated messages. Since that time, humans have been asking questions about the meaning of those messages. Our curiosity, our questioning, and our ability to reflect on our own thinking are core to our success as a species. And our ability to analyze ourselves, our actions, and our impacts will be essential for our ability to sustain our civilization. Teaching our students to decode their world is not just a nice 21st century educational objective. It is a necessity; it is fundamental to our role as "teachers"; and it is core to our human vocation.

In March 2018, Chris gave a 90-minute presentation to 50 teachers and teacher trainers in Istanbul. This event occurred at a particularly tumultuous time in Turkey. A failed coup attempt had been followed by a crackdown on the press and on liberal education, with more than 20,000 teachers being fired. At the end of Chris's presentation, a teacher jumped up and shouted, "If we teach the way this man is saying, if we teach our students to continually ask questions, we could be fired or worse!" Without a pause, a second teacher jumped up and proclaimed, "If we do not teach our students to ask questions, then we are not teaching them at all." The room erupted with intense debate for the next 30 minutes on the risks and the imperatives of media literacy education.

Although there are risks in teaching students to think critically in the United States today, we still have democratic privileges that allow us to teach our students to ask questions (at least some questions) without risking our jobs or our safety. Although we grapple with the limits of time and resources, the overwhelming needs of our students and communities, and the day-to-day burdens of our endless responsibilities as educators, the struggles of our Turkish colleagues can help to remind us of the ideals of our work. Inquiry and reflection are at the core of media literacy... and at the heart of what it means to be human.

REFERENCES

Alvermann, D. E., & Hagood, M. C. (2010). Critical media literacy: Research, theory, and practice in "new times." *Journal of Education Research, 93*(3), 193–205.

Appiah, K. A. (2020, June 18). The case for capitalizing the B in black. *The Atlantic.* www.theatlantic.com/ideas/archive/2020/06/time-to-capitalize-black and-white/613159

Arthur, J., Davies, I., & Hahn, C. (Eds.). (2008). *The SAGE handbook of education for citizenship and democracy.* Thousand Oaks, CA: Sage.

Aufderheide, P. (1993). *Media literacy: A report of the National Leadership Conference on Media Literacy.* Queenstown, MD: Aspen Institute.

Aufderheide, P., & Jaszi, P. (2018). *Reclaiming fair use: How to put balance back in copyright* (2nd ed.). Chicago: University of Chicago Press.

Bergsma, L., Considine, D., Culver, S. H., Hobbs, R., Jensen, A., Rogow, F., et al. (2007). *Core principles of media literacy education in the United States* [Policy report]. New York: National Association for Media Literacy Education.

Beschloss, M. (2016, May 7). The ad that helped Reagan sell good times to an uncertain nation. *New York Times.* www.nytimes.com/2016/05/08/business/the-ad-that-helped-reagan-sell-good-times-to-an-uncertain-nation.html

Birkett, T. (1994). *The Truax.* Wood Flooring Manufacturers Association.

Browne, M. N., & Keeley, S. M. (2014). *Asking the right questions: A guide to critical thinking* (11th ed.). Hoboken, NJ: Pearson.

Common Core State Standards Initiative. (2021). *English language arts standards.* www.corestandards.org/ELA-Literacy

Common Sense Media. (2015). *The Common Sense census: Media use by tweens and teens.* www.commonsensemedia.org/sites/default/files/uploads/research/census_researchreport.pdf

Common Sense Media. (2019). *The Common Sense census: Media use by tweens and teens in 2019.* www.commonsensemedia.org/research/the-common-sense-census-media-use-by-tweens-and-teens-2019

Condliffe, B., Quint, J., Visher, M. G., Bangser, M. R., Drohojowska, S., Saco, L., et al. (2017). *Project-based learning: A literature review* [Working paper]. New York: MDRC.

Condry, J. (1989). *The psychology of television.* New York: Routledge.

Considine, D. M., & Baker, F. (2006). Focus on film: Learning through the movies. *Middle Ground, 10*(2), 12–15.

Democracy Ready NY. (2020). *Developing digital citizens: Media literacy education for all students.* www.democracyreadyny.org/Developing-Digital-Citizens-Final-for-Website2.pdf

Freire, A. M. A., & Macedo, D. (Eds.). (1998). *The Paulo Freire reader.* New York: Cassell and Continuum.

Freire, P. (1970). *Pedagogy of the oppressed.* New York: Herder & Herder.

Freire, P. (1985). *The politics of education: Culture, power, and liberation.* Westport, CT: Bergin & Garvey.

Friesem, E. (2014). A story of conflict and collaboration: Media literacy, video production and disadvantaged youth. *Journal of Media Literacy Education, 6*(1), 44–55. https://digitalcommons.uri.edu/cgi/viewcontent.cgi?article=1140&context=jmle

Funk, S. S., Kellner, D., & Share, J. (2016). Critical media literacy as transformative pedagogy. In M. N. Yildiz & J. Keengwe (Eds.), *Handbook of research on media literacy in the digital age* (pp. 1–30). Hershey, PA: IGI Global.

Hobbs, R. (2010a). *Copyright clarity: How fair use supports digital learning.* Thousand Oaks, CA: Corwin.

Hobbs, R. (2010b). *Digital and media literacy: A plan of action.* Washington, DC: Aspen Institute.

Jenkins, H. (2009). *Confronting the challenges of participatory culture: Media education for the 21st century* [White paper]. Chicago: MacArthur Foundation. www.macfound.org/media/article_pdfs/jenkins_white_paper.pdf

Kahne, J., & Bowyer, B. (2017). Educating for democracy in a partisan age: Confronting the challenges of motivated reasoning and misinformation. *American Educational Research Journal, 54*(1), 3–34.

Kendi, I. X. (2019). *How to be an antiracist.* New York: One World.

Kozulin, A., Gindis, B., Ageyev, V. S., & Miller, S. M. (Eds.). (2003). *Vygotsky's educational theory in cultural context.* New York: Cambridge University Press.

Madda, M. J. (2019, May 15). Dena Simmons: Without context, social-emotional learning can backfire. *EdSurge.* www.edsurge.com/news/2019-05-15-dena-simmons-without-context-social-emotional-learning-can-backfire

McLuhan, M. (1994). *Understanding media: The extensions of man.* Cambridge, MA: MIT Press.

McTighe, J., & Silver, H. F. (2020). *Teaching for deeper learning: Tools to engage students in meaning making.* Alexandria, VA: ASCD.

Media Literacy Now. (2021). *Resources for educators and librarians.* https://medialiteracynow.org/resources-for-teachers

National Archives at Boston. (2021). *Trial of the century: La Amistad.* www.archives.gov/boston/featured-documents/amistad-warrant.html

National Association for Media Literacy Education (NAMLE). (2020). *Media literacy defined.* https://namle.net/resources/media-literacy-defined

National Association for Media Literacy Education (NAMLE). (2021). *Learn how to access, analyze, evaluate, create, and act using all forms of communication.* https://namle.net/resources

National Council for the Social Studies (NCSS). (2021). *College, career, and civic life (C3) framework for Social Studies State Standards.* www.socialstudies.org/standards/c3

National Museum of African American History and Culture. (2021). *Talking about race: Being antiracist.* https://nmaahc.si.edu/learn/talking-about-race/topics/being-antiracist

National Science Teachers Association (NSTA). (2021). *Access the Next Generation Science Standards by topic.* https://ngss.nsta.org/accessstandardsbytopic.aspx

New York Performance Standards Consortium. (2020). *A better way to assess student learning.* www.performanceassessment.org

New York State Education Department (NYSED). (2004). *Regents high school examination: Global history and geography.* Office of State Assessment. www.nysedregents.org/globalhistorygeography/Archive/20040617exam.pdf

PBS. (1999). *American photography: A century of images. Part 4* [Video recording].

Scheibe, C. (2018). Piaget and Pokémon: What can theories of developmental psychology tell us about children and media? In N. A. Jennings & S. R. Mazzarella (Eds.), *20 questions about youth and the media* (Rev. ed., pp. 61–72). New York: Peter Lang.

Scheibe, C., & Rogow, F. (2012). *The teacher's guide to media literacy: Critical thinking in a multimedia world.* Thousand Oaks, CA: Corwin.

Seuss, Dr. (1971). *The Lorax.* New York: Random House.

Shafer, R. G. (2016). *Carnival campaign: How the rollicking 1840 campaign of "Tippecanoe and Tyler Too" changed presidential elections forever.* Chicago: Chicago Review Press.

Sperry, C., LaZarre, C., & Mayer, M. (2008). *Introducing Africa: Critical thinking and media literacy.* Ithaca, NY: Project Look Sharp.

Sperry, C., & Scheibe, C. (2018). Resolving copyright concerns in the development of diverse curriculum materials for media analysis activities. In R. Hobbs (Ed.), *The Routledge companion to media education, copyright, and fair use* (pp. 274–291). New York: Routledge.

Sperry, C., & Scheibe, C. (2020). Rx for an infodemic: Media decoding, COVID-19 and online teaching. *Social Education, 84*(3), 152–158.

Sperry, S. (2014). Sustainability education and media literacy. *Green Teacher, 104,* 8–11.

Starr, P. (2004). *The creation of the media: Political origins of modern communications.* New York: Basic Books.

Wiggins, G., & McTighe, J. (2005). *Understanding by design.* Alexandria, VA: ASCD.

World Economic Forum. (2020). *This is how COVID-19 has changed media habits in each generation.* www.weforum.org/agenda/2020/04/covid19-media-consumption-generation-pandemic-entertainment

World Health Organization. (2020, February 2). *Novel coronavirus (2019-nCoV) situation report.*

Wright, L. (2019, September 3). Like Frederick Douglass, our freedom stories start with education. *Project Forever Free: Liberty Through Learning.* https://projectforeverfree.org/like-frederick-douglass-our-freedom-stories-start-with-education

INDEX

Note: Page references followed by an italicized *f* indicates information contained in figures.

ABOUT THE AUTHORS

 **Chris Sperry** is cofounder and director of curriculum and staff development of Project Look Sharp at Ithaca College. He taught middle and high school social studies, English, and media studies at the Lehman Alternative Community School in Ithaca, New York, for more than 40 years, where he also served as an instructional coach and a mentor for teachers. He is the author and coauthor of many articles, lessons, and curriculum kits for integrating media literacy and critical thinking into the K–12 curriculum. He has delivered hundreds of media literacy workshops, classes, and keynote addresses for educators throughout the United States and around the world. Chris was the recipient of the National Council for the Social Studies 2008 Award for Global Understanding and the 2005 National PTA and Cable's Leaders in Learning Award for Media Literacy. He earned a Bachelor of Arts degree from Ithaca College with a planned studies major in media literacy and a master's degree in human development from Harvard University.

 **Cyndy Scheibe** is cofounder and executive director of Project Look Sharp at Ithaca College, where she is also a professor of psychology, teaching courses in child and adolescent development, media literacy, and media effects; she also coordinates the college's interdisciplinary media literacy minor. She was a founding board member of the National Association for Media Literacy Education and coauthored the association's Core Principles of Media Literacy Education. Her publications on media literacy education include ASCD's

Quick Reference Guide *Media Literacy in Every Classroom* and *The Teacher's Guide to Media Literacy: Critical Thinking in a Multimedia World*, both coauthored with Faith Rogow; and the book chapter "Piaget and Pókemon: What Can the Theories of Developmental Psychology Tell Us About Children and Media?" in *20 Questions About Youth and the Media*. She has a master's degree in communications and a PhD in developmental psychology, both from Cornell University.

Related ASCD Resources: Media Literacy and Critical Thinking

At the time of publication, the following resources were available (ASCD stock numbers appear in parentheses).

Print Products

A Close Look at Close Reading: Teaching Students to Analyze Complex Texts, Grades K–5 by Diane Lapp, Barbara Moss, Maria Grant, and Kelly Johnson (#114008)

Complex Text Decoded: How to Design Lessons and Use Strategies That Target Authentic Texts by Kathy T. Glass (#115006)

Cultivating Curiosity in K–12 Classrooms: How to Promote and Sustain Deep Learning by Wendy L. Ostroff (#116001)

EdTech Essentials: The Top 10 Technology Strategies for All Learning Environments by Monica Burns (#121021)

Engaging Students in Reading All Types of Text (Quick Reference Guide) by Pam Allyn and Monica Burns (#QRG121059)

The Fundamentals of Understanding by Design (Quick Reference Guide) by Jay McTighe (#QRG117084)

The i5 Approach: Lesson Planning That Teaches Thinking and Fosters Innovation by Jane E. Pollock with Susan Hensley (#117030)

Making Curriculum Matter: How to Build SEL, Equity, and Other Priorities into Daily Instruction by Angela Di Michele Lalor (#122007)

Media Literacy in Every Classroom (Quick Reference Guide) by Faith Rogow and Cyndy Scheibe (#QRG117107)

Questioning for Classroom Discussion: Purposeful Speaking, Engaged Listening, Deep Thinking by Jackie Acree Walsh and Beth Dankert Sattes (#115012)

Researching in a Digital World: How do I teach my students to conduct quality online research (ASCD Arias) by Erik Palmer (#SF115051)

Rise to the Challenge: Designing Rigorous Learning That Maximizes Student Success by Jeff C. Marshall (#120007)

Teaching for Deeper Learning: Tools to Engage Students in Meaning Making by Jay McTighe and Harvey F. Silver (#120022)

What If? Building Students' Problem-Solving Skills Through Complex Challenges by Ronald A. Beghetto (#118009)

For up-to-date information about ASCD resources, go to **www.ascd.org.** You can search the complete archives of *Educational Leadership* at **www.ascd.org/el.**

ASCD myTeachSource®

Download resources from a professional learning platform with hundreds of research-based best practices and tools for your classroom at http://myteachsource.ascd.org/.

For more information, send an e-mail to member@ascd.org; call 1-800-933-2723 or 703-578-9600; send a fax to 703-575-5400; or write to Information Services, ASCD, 1703 N. Beauregard St., Alexandria, VA 22311-1714 USA.

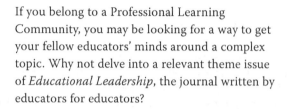

CPSIA information can be obtained
at www.ICGtesting.com
Printed in the USA
LVHW081443260322
714487LV00014B/264